Lisa catches me at the lockers and she's brimming with something.

'Okay, today's the day. I can feel it,' she says, leaning against the wall. 'Steven's going to ask me out, for sure.'

I close my locker and she straightens up.

'God, what's the matter with you? You look like shit.'

I shake my head as the bell grinds out the time. Five minutes to get to our form rooms. We duck into the loos.

'Are you sick?' Lisa stands behind me as I grip the basin and look at myself in the mirror. 'Or are you just in one of your moods again?'

I look up at her. 'I am *not* moody.'

'You are so. You're one of the moodiest people I know. You never used to be like this.' She examines her teeth in the mirror, checking for bits of breakfast, then glances back at me, obviously waiting for some kind of explanation.

'Yeah, well, right now I just hate my life, okay?' I look at my mouth speaking the words. 'I really, really hate my life.'

TA Blezard's first novel, *Mohan Alone*, was published in 1988. Since then she has written four non-fiction books in the Mysterious World series and another for the Hodder Wayland series on space. She now spends her time teaching English, writing and looking after her parrot. *Secrets* is her second novel.

SECRETS

TA Blezard

Livewire

First published by Livewire Books, The Women's Press Ltd, 2002
A member of the Namara Group
34 Great Sutton Street, London EC1V 0LQ
www.the-womens-press.com

Copyright © Tracey Blezard 2002

The right of TA Blezard to be identified as the author of this work has been asserted by her in accordance with the Copyright, Designs and Patents Act 1988.

British Library Cataloguing-in-Publication Data
A catalogue record for this book is available from the British Library.

This book is sold subject to the condition that it shall not, by way of trade or otherwise, be lent, re-sold, hired out, or otherwise circulated without the Publisher's prior consent in any form of binding or cover other than that in which it is published and without a similar condition including this condition being imposed on the subsequent purchaser.

ISBN 0 7043 4977 9

Typeset in 12/14pt Bembo by FiSH Books, London WC1
Printed and bound in Great Britain by Cox & Wyman, Reading, Berkshire

For Lucy

One

The first time my stepfather laid a hand on me I was secretly glad. I remember thinking, now something is finally going to change. Now Mum will *have* to do something. But she just looked at me with hollow eyes and told me not to answer back. Colin worked hard for the three of us. He worked hard to provide us with all the nice things we had, our nice little life. He didn't deserve to come home after a long day and get lip off some 'jumped-up teenager' in a mood. Apparently.

Before then I had never realised it was *them* against *me*. I'd always thought Mum and I were on the same side. Especially when Colin had been drinking and flew into one of his rages. But suddenly everything seemed different – I was on the outside for the first time in my life.

Of course the incident was quickly forgotten, filed away with all the other fragments, hidden behind great bear hugs, tears, apologies and wild promises. In the end, I let it go. I had to. Colin didn't exactly make a habit of hitting me or my brother David, so I felt I must have deserved it in some way, for pushing him that bit too far.

I've always felt like there's a hidden part of me that's dark and mysterious – a piece of my *real* father which makes me do and say things I shouldn't, say things to make Colin mad. I'm not sure.

My real dad vanished overnight when I was eight years old. I remember very little about the time before he left. We were just like everyone else, I suppose. An ordinary family. Then one morning we woke up to find that Dad had gone, just like that, and no one talked about him any more. Something terrible had happened, that was all I knew.

My mother changed after that. Her skin became strained across her face, her eyes wide and panicky. She cried herself to sleep every night for months and David and I were too scared to ask why. An infectious fear seeped through the house, a fear that somehow we were exposed to all the bad things that were out there.

Perhaps that's the reason why Mum bounced like a pinball through a series of boyfriends over the next few years. Some of them I remember; others were just figures in cars, honking the horn for her to come out of the house while David and I peeped curiously from behind the curtains. Some even became a part of our lives. Like brain-dead Bob who used to bring David and me sweets and send us off to the cinema for the afternoon. I remember he took us all to see *Cinderella* in panto once. Then he moved in and left his dirty socks in the bathroom, and stuffed crumpled newspapers down the sides of our armchairs. A year later he too was gone, just another of the names that Mum would sometimes drop into conversation and then just as easily drop all together. I watched her boyfriends come and go, wondering which of them would eventually stay and become our new dad.

The position was finally filled when Colin came on to the scene. Colin Bliss. Bliss by name and bliss by nature Mum used to say. He took us for long drives in the country in his brand new Volvo and bought Mum expensive presents. Even paid for us all to go abroad on holiday. He said how lucky he was to have a ready-made family; that he was too old to be dealing with babies and youngsters. We were just what he wanted, or so he said. Mum proudly dolled herself up, fluttering around him like a butterfly, cooking his favourite dishes, pressing his pin-striped shirts.

I was twelve when they got married. I was so happy. Colin was the kind of dad you secretly dreamed of – the kind of dad I had always assumed our real father would turn out to be. In my eyes he could do no wrong. He always made out like he didn't understand twelve-year-old girls but he understood much more than he ever let on. He pretended not to know about music or fashion or stuff like that but then he would surprise me with a present, and it was always something I'd been absolutely dying for. He knew exactly how to get round me. David was more sceptical but then David was fourteen and pretty much hated everything and everyone, including me.

So my mother was married in a registry office with a blood-red carpet and we officially moved into Col's house and into his life. 'Just like a proper family again,' smiled Mum. Colin would look after us, and wipe out all the bad times. He had an important job in the investment world, wore black braces over a pale blue shirt with a stiff white collar, and on good days would come home with two bottles of champagne in his pink shovel hands.

And there were plenty of good times in that first year. That's why it was such a shock when one day, for no apparent reason, he got so mad that he punched a hole in the kitchen door. His anger just came out of nowhere and it left me and David and Mum speechless, waiting for him to explain and make everything right again.

Colin was good at explaining things. He would shout when he'd had a hard day at work, when things hadn't gone the way he wanted. We didn't understand the kind of pressure he was under, Mum told us patiently. One time, after someone had carved him up in the car, he threw a blue china vase across the room and it smashed against the wall just behind Mum's head. I don't know who was more shocked: him or Mum. He broke down in tears and sobbed his sorries into her neck. 'Can you still love me?' he blubbed. 'You're too good for me, Miriam, you and the kids. I don't deserve you. I keep thinking that one day you'll all walk out and leave me.' And of course Mum knew that pain all too well. She just melted and it was all forgotten. Over. Done.

I guess everyone goes through bad patches. It's just that after a while it seemed like I was counting the good times, not the bad, hanging out for it to get better, the way it was in the beginning. But things were tough at work. People didn't want to buy into Colin's lucrative investment deals. He started coming home later and later, after drowning his sorrows in wine bars across town. He said it was hard work keeping Mum in the manner to which she'd become accustomed. And sometimes the angry words would lead to furniture being thrown, muffled cries and thumps from downstairs after David and I had gone to bed.

But it wasn't always like that.

It *isn't* always like that.

They've been married for almost four years now but it seems longer. I'm sixteen. Doing GCSEs, with mocks coming up in a couple of months. David is eighteen going on nineteen. He works in a garage fitting tyres all day and still acts like he hates the whole world.

Mum tells me she and Colin are happy. That all couples have their ups and downs. I don't know if I believe her. She won't accept that Colin's moods are getting worse and she doesn't see how he's changed her – she doesn't wear make-up any more because he's told her it makes her look cheap, she hardly goes out any more, and never sees anyone unless she's okayed it with him first. But she's happy. Happy that he criticises her, her clothes, her cooking, happy that he blames her when *I* do something wrong. And when Mum runs upstairs sobbing into a wad of kitchen towel, Colin just turns to me or David and says 'Your mother's weak, she can't take criticism.' Criticism is his way of building you up, of showing you your mistakes. I don't know, but I'm starting to think that Mum's only mistake was marrying him in the first place.

Two

This afternoon I am free to walk over to my mate Lisa's place before going home. It's not something I do very often these days but we have homework to finish and, besides, I know that Colin has a meeting and definitely won't be home until eight. He likes us all to sit down and have dinner together when he gets back from work. (That's *if* he gets back at all – sometimes we just sit around waiting for him and he turns up at eleven and goes straight to bed. But then that's Colin's privilege as head of the household. Heaven forbid that I should behave in the same way.)

I explain my curfew to Lisa almost without thinking, striving as always to sound casual. I have grown used to making excuses so that no one will find out how things *really* are. Lisa just flicks back her sleek black hair.

'It's okay. Stay as long as you like. You used to be over here all the time when we were kids. Now I hardly ever see you.' She shoots me a glance. 'I was beginning to think I'm not good enough for you.'

'What's that supposed to mean?' I look up sharply.

She shrugs. 'Well, you know, in that big old house of your stepdad's and everything. Maybe you think coming round here is slumming it or something.'

'It's just a house. A house doesn't change anything,' I say, stiffly.

She shrugs again, obviously embarrassed to have brought it up.

'I was just kidding.' She shuffles the papers in front of her and changes the subject. 'So which'll we do first? Physics or geography?'

Mrs Stanley comes through with a tray of biscuits, juice, crisps and cheese on crackers and places them on the dining-room table in front of us.

'Brain food,' she smiles and wafts back out again.

Lisa rolls her eyes. 'Not surprising I can't lose any weight.'

'You still dieting?'

'Naa, well, on and off. Mum's dead set against it. She's always telling me I can't study properly if I'm starving.'

'I guess.' She dives for a cheesy cracker and I timidly follow her lead. I chew each mouthful until it disintegrates in my mouth, making one biscuit last as long as four of Lisa's. I don't want to ruin my appetite for dinner.

'Relax, will you?' Lisa gobbles up her biscuit, watching me closely. 'You seem all on edge these days. What's up?'

I just shake my head dismissively. I can't help but hold myself tightly. I've been doing it for months, holding everything in so no one sees my life is falling apart. I wish Lisa hadn't noticed. She knows I've changed, however hard I try to pretend that I'm still good old Briony Newman. I glance at my watch, calculating how long it will be before I can get away.

Don't get me wrong. It's not that I don't like spending time with Lisa. She's my best mate and has been for years. I guess it's just easier when we're in school. In the last year and a half school has become my haven. I feel safe there.

Outside it's like being in free fall – there are too many things that can go wrong.

Lisa reaches across the table to my geography project and flips through the folder.

'God, Bri, look at all the work you've done already. I haven't even written up my objectives yet. I can't think what to put. My only objective is to pass, but I can't write that.'

'Yeah, well, I only regurgitated what Mr Stevens told us. It's all pretty vague really.'

She laughs. 'I can't even *remember* what he told us. Jesus, I wish I was more like you. I might have some hope of a decent grade then.'

I smile. Lisa be more like me? Is she out of her tiny mind? As far as school is concerned, Lisa is one of those people who always manages to scrape by, regardless of how little work she does. She'll leave all her revision until the very last minute, cram for one night, fret about it the next day, and then ace it. Me, I have to work hard for my fairly mediocre grades. People like her don't deserve to do well, Colin says. It's luck he reckons. There's no substitute for good, honest, hard work. He's worked hard all his life, he tells us over and over again.

After an hour of trying to make sense of the stats our class collected on a day out in town interviewing passers-by about public transport and the benefits of the new Winterbourne shopping complex, Lisa and I have had enough. We slip upstairs and she sticks on a CD, then pulls open her make-up drawer and gazes contentedly inside.

'I got this yesterday lunch-time with Francine and Aysha.' She winds up the lipstick in her hand. 'I'd have asked you to come, but you were out *running*.'

Running is one of my more un-cool pursuits but I still force myself to do it although I don't even do it very well. My PE teacher tells me I need to pace myself more if I want to run distances but I just sprint until my muscles burn, my lungs feel as though they're about to explode, and I can't concentrate on anything except the pain. Somehow that makes me feel better.

'Where d'you get all the money from anyway?' I say, glancing up from the pages of one of Lisa's mags.

'Same as you. Same as everyone. *Mummy and Daddy*.'

'Francine's got a part-time job, hasn't she?'

'Yeah, I know. Maybe I should get one. Think of all the stuff I could buy.'

'I don't know why you shove all that gunk on your face anyway,' I mutter from behind the pages of an article entitled 'How to spot the signs your man is cheating on you'.

'Oh yeah, like you'd be adverse to a bit of eyeliner,' Lisa scoffs, outlining her lips with her latest acquisition.

I think Lisa is beautiful, make-up or no make-up. Her hair is straight to her shoulders and inky black, and her eyes are green and sharp, always looking for something she can take the piss out of, searching out a joke or a laugh. When I tell her she is pretty, she insists that I am much prettier than she is, as if it's some kind of competition. Then she goes on about how she doesn't know why I haven't got a boyfriend yet, as if that's the ultimate measure of prettiness.

'There're plenty of boys that are interested,' she informs me each time.

'Yeah, a bunch of creeps,' comes my standard reply.

I know it's probably not true, about them being creeps, but sometimes it's easier to say that than get into some lengthy discussion about it all.

Lisa swivels round from the dressing table and looks hard at me.

'We are mates, aren't we?'

I look back at her, surprised. 'Well, yeah, course we are.'

'And you would tell me if there was anything... you know, wrong? I mean, we don't have any secrets or anything. We tell each other everything, right?'

It's true. Lisa told me the first time she smoked a cigarette, the first time she really kissed a boy and the first time they got to what she called 'second base'. But I've been holding out on her. I feel my heart quicken.

'You know we do. Honest, there's nothing I haven't told you, nothing's up.'

(Funny how, when you're about to tell someone a lie, you always start with the word 'honest'.)

Lisa goes back to brushing this fake tan stuff over her cheeks but I sense there is more to come.

'You just seem so distant these days,' she mutters, into the mirror.

I'm aware that she feels I've abandoned her recently and I do feel guilty about it.

'Yeah, well, not everyone is as touchy, feely, gushy-gushy as you, you know Lise,' I say trying to lighten things up.

'I just thought something might be bothering you, that's all. You know if something *is* bugging you, you can always tell me. I'm a good listener.'

'D'you want me to make something up just to keep you happy?'

'If you like.' She reaches into the drawer again.

'Okay.' I close the magazine, roll onto my back, and stare up at the ceiling. 'I've been seeing this boy for six months now and I think he's cheating on me.'

'Yeah, right,' Lisa grumbles. 'What boy? There's no scandal attached to your name, Miss Purer than Pure. If you're going to lie, at least make it semi-believable. Hey, you know what though? I was thinking, maybe we could double date.'

I sit upright. 'Excuse me? With who? When?'

'Well, me and Steven have been getting on quite well lately. I think we could be taking it to the next level pretty soon and I just thought if he asks me out on a date, maybe you could come too. We could make it a foursome.'

'You what? Are you serious? A foursome with who?'

'Ian, of course.'

Ian and Steven are in our tutor group. I've never really thought of them as anything other than schoolfriends, but Lisa obviously has.

'It could be fun. What d'you reckon?'

'I reckon you're mad. I reckon I don't need you to organise my love life for me.'

'You're absolutely sure about that?' Lisa raises an eyebrow.

'But I don't even know Ian.'

She makes a snorting noise and tosses her head back. 'You see him every day at school. You have done for years.'

'Yeah, but I never saw him... like *that*, you know.'

'So? He hasn't got two heads. He's nice enough looking. He's a good laugh. And anyway, I'm not asking you to marry him.'

'Come on, you don't want me crowding you with Sexy Steve,' I tease her.

'You won't be crowding me,' Lisa replies patiently. 'It'll be a *four*some.'

If I make too big a deal of this, I'm going to end up looking really sad so I just shrug my shoulders and let it go.

'Yeah, well, *if* you even get that far, then we'll see. I suppose it could be worse.'

'Yeah – it could be Martin Foster,' Lisa says and we both laugh cruelly. (Martin Foster is a nerd of the highest order.) 'Anyway, maybe things won't go according to plan. Maybe Steven's just being friendly, the way he is with everyone. Maybe I've misread the signs.'

She turns back to the mirror, shuffling along the stool to make room for me. We both sit there and examine our numerous imperfections. Lisa waves a cover stick in my direction.

'Let me make you over.'

'I don't like all that stuff.'

'Go on, it'll be a laugh.' She rummages in her drawer of delights and pulls out some lippy, winding it up for me to see. 'This'd really suit your colouring. I'm too dark for it.'

Colin says only whores wear lipstick. I know it isn't true but stuff like that can really stick in your mind sometimes. I'm sure he works with loads of high-powered women who wear make-up and I bet he doesn't call them whores.

'Here, use this,' Lisa hands me a tiny brush.

'What's this for?'

'Make-up artists always use a brush. Come on, let me.'

She turns to face me and gently starts to paint on the lip colour.

'I reckon I'd be a good make-up artist. What do you think? Pout.'

I pout.

'I thought you were planning on going to university?' I ask her.

She stops brushing my lips and frowns. 'I was only joking, Bri. I don't really want to spend my life painting famous people's faces so *they* can look good instead of me.' She puts the brush to my mouth again. 'You take everything so seriously sometimes.'

She spends about ten minutes doing my eyes and follows this with a light dusting of powder across my cheekbones. When she's finished, I glance down at my watch. It's barely six but suddenly I feel I've stayed too long.

'I've got to go.'

Lisa squints over at her alarm clock. 'It's early yet.'

'Yeah, I know, but I should give Mum a hand before Col gets home.'

'Aah, aren't you good? Are you sure your name isn't secretly Walton?' she quips. 'Goodnight, John-Boy, goodnight, Mary Ellen, goodnight *Briony*.'

'Why d'you always have to be like that?' I say irritably stuffing things back into my bag.

'Like what? What did I say? You didn't have a sense of humour bypass during the holidays by any chance?'

'No. Did you?'

'Dunno. Maybe. *You* don't seem to find me funny any more.'

'Yeah, well, I really should go.' I crack a forced smile. 'I can't waste all my time listening to your crap jokes.'

'Thanks, *mate*.' Lisa snorts.

As she walks me to the front door, her mum pops her head out of the kitchen to ask if I'd like to stay for tea.

'It's fish cakes,' she says, enticingly.

Lisa rolls her eyes. I decline politely and slip out into the watery September sunshine. All I can concentrate on is getting back and washing this stuff off my face before Colin sees it.

Three

'Is that you, love?' My mother's small voice quivers from the kitchen and before the front door has even closed behind me she is standing in the hall.

'Oh, it's only you Briony,' she sighs, then catches sight of the cack on my face. 'For God's sake, girl, what *do* you think you're playing at coming home looking like that? Go upstairs and wash it off.' She turns back to the kitchen, muttering under her breath while I slope off to the bathroom.

Poor old Mum, I think, as I splash cold water over my face. I feel angry with myself, as if I've let her down. I should have insisted on taking the make-up off before I left the Stanleys' place. But then what would Lisa have thought? I towel off and look at my plain, scrubbed face in the mirror. Slightly sandy, slightly freckly. Nothing much there for Ian to fancy, I reckon.

In the kitchen I peel vegetables as Mum checks on a casserole that's bubbling in the oven.

'I hope he's not early. This needs another hour at least.'

'So, he'll just have to wait for his tea like the rest of us,' I mumble to the potato in my hand.

Mum asks if I've had a good time at Lisa's. I tell her we did homework and she leaves it at that. Being a good wife to Colin seems to exhaust her these days and though she asks me questions about school and friends, she doesn't really hear the answers any more, too tired to think of anything except keeping the house straight, and making sure things are all in their proper place, just the way Colin likes them.

And she's got plenty to keep straight. The house has four bedrooms, two bathrooms, a double garage, a large garden, a fitted kitchen, and matching carpet throughout, even in the downstairs loo. The place is full of expensive paintings, vases, ornaments, handwoven rugs and golf trophies. We want for nothing in this house thanks to Colin and his investment deals. Mum tells us how lucky we are to have such nice things and she's probably right. I'm sure that my own father would never have provided for us the way Colin has. The fact that he vanished from our lives so completely is proof of that.

Mum doesn't work, so everything we have is because of Colin. She even gets a different car each year when Colin replaces his own and gives her his old one. Not that she has driven in over eight months, mind. Colin took the keys away one day and she's never got them back. These are privileges that have to be *earned*, he says. Mum tells me she's not bothered.

'I was never a good driver anyway, Bri,' she confides. 'I'm happier without a car to be perfectly honest.'

'But you could get out more if you drove.'

'And go where?' She laughs a tight laugh.

One hour later Mum takes the casserole out for another look. It smells great, the gravy just crusting around the edge of the dish. We hear Colin's car come rolling up the drive and Mum heaves a huge sigh of relief.

'Perfect,' she whispers to herself. Some nights everything just falls into place.

'Something smells nice,' Colin calls jovially from the hallway and a second later he's there in the kitchen as Mum hastily double-checks the table. 'Are we eating in here?'

'Well, yes, I... I thought we might,' stutters Mum in her usual mousy voice. 'I can move things into the dining room if you'd prefer. It's no bother.'

'No, no, here'll do.'

I feel a familiar knot tightening in my stomach. Col falls into his chair at the kitchen table, takes off his jacket and undoes his cufflinks, filling up the room. He asks how his two favourite girls are but doesn't really expect an answer. Mum lays the casserole in front of him while I hover in the background with the vegetables.

'And where's The Boy David?'

For some unknown reason this is how Colin refers to my brother.

'He... he's not back yet,' Mum replies in a breathy whisper and the knot tightens under my belt. 'I expect the bus is caught in traffic again.'

My stepfather mutters something, gets up, grabs himself a beer from the fridge then sits back down again, still grumbling. There's something strange going on these days between David and Colin. David is older now and in the last few years he's grown up and filled out a fair bit. Maybe that's why he gets away with things. Or maybe Colin realises that David just doesn't care any more. You can't get to someone who doesn't give a toss.

'Shall we wait for him?' Mum asks.

'If he can't get his arse to the table on time, that's his lookout.'

I sense Colin's not happy about my brother's absence but he's going to let it go. Mum spoons casserole and mash carefully onto his plate and the three of us settle down to eat.

Barely five minutes later, the front door slams and David slinks into view. My brother is tall and blond, with hollow cheeks, green eyes, and an endless string of pathetic girlfriends to his name.

'You're late.' Colin eyes David coldly.

'Bus was late.' David stands in the doorway, not brazen enough just to plonk himself down, but late just the same. He scratches at his arms like a monkey.

'You'd better apologise to your mother after she's gone to the trouble of cooking,' Colin says in that dangerous, flat monotone of his. Like Colin has ever apologised for coming in late. Bloody hypocrite.

'Oh no, it really isn't...' Mum starts but Colin cuts her off.

'Let the boy apologise, Miriam.' His voice is firm. He turns back to David. 'Well?'

'Yeah, sorry, Mum,' David says, staring straight through her.

Mum smiles that tired, guarded smile of hers, already getting up to fetch the plate she left warming on the hob.

'There.' Colin speaks into his dinner without looking up but somehow he knows that everyone is listening. 'Now we can just sit down and enjoy a nice family meal.'

Maybe it's all in my head. Maybe it's just worse thinking of what *might* happen than dealing with what actually *does* happen. I push the casserole around my plate, forcing lumps of it down without tasting it. I hate meal times. I'm sure I'm getting an ulcer.

It's late, but I'm itching to burn off some of this cold energy that builds up when I'm stuck in the house. As Mum and Colin relax in the front room and David does whatever it is he does in his bedroom for hours on end I pull my sports kit out of my bag and sniff dubiously at the armpits. I can probably get another run out of it, just to clear my head.

I slip out the back door and get into my stride, blitzing past the drinkers who fall out of the pub on North Bridge Road. My breathing is desperate, not the steady, regular pattern of a proper athlete. I can feel the tension burning in my muscles and my throat is raw but I push myself harder, pick up the pace, feel the sweat running down the back of my neck and the cool drizzle on my face. After a while there is nothing else.

When the pain finally gets the better of me I double over and let my body relax for a moment, catching my breath. Above me the clouds clear to reveal a pale, slender moon and somewhere far beyond that, the pinpricks of distant stars. I look at them, as I always do, wondering how they can exist so very far away, almost like they belong to another dimension. Hard to remember that we are all part of the same universe.

As I slink silently back into the house I glance through the open door to the living room and see Mum massaging Colin's heavy shoulders. He rolls his head from side to side in ecstasy, like a cat getting a belly scratch.

'Ooh, that's so good, Miriam.'

I pause, momentarily mesmerised by this tender picture of togetherness. Colin's eyes open and lock on to mine.

'Where've you been?' He straightens up in his chair. 'It's far too late for you to be out.'

His voice is more suspicious than angry but I can feel my heart pounding as I edge into the doorway.

'I just went for a run.'

Mum sits on the arm of his chair looking at me. I stare back, wondering if this is going to matter tonight, if this is going to trigger anything. I can tell that Colin is deciding the same thing.

'Yes, well, just make sure you ask next time,' he snorts. 'It's not good for young girls to be out on their own without telling anyone. You never know what could happen.'

I nod. 'Yeah, I will. Sorry.'

The words are hollow. I'm not sorry at all and he probably knows it. He turns back to Mum, slips his arm round her hips and gives her a conspiratorial squeeze.

'We don't want her getting too muscly, do we, Miriam? Men don't like women with big muscles.'

I shoot him a watery smile of acknowledgement, then escape back to the sanctuary of my bedroom.

Maybe men don't like women with muscles because they can hit back.

Showered and sliding between the cool covers of my bed I can feel my body ache from the hard workout it's been given. This is the best time of all. I am too tired to worry. I will fall asleep with my face in the pages of a book and with any luck not think about anything else till morning.

Four

Breakfast is a hurried affair Monday to Friday. As I dash down the stairs I can smell clouds of Colin's aftershave wafting around after his shower.

'Is there more toast?' I eye David taking one of Col's slices.

'There's bread in the bin. Make your father some more as well.' There's a hint of irritation behind Mum's words as she notices what David has done, yet she continues making his sandwiches for lunch as if he is some helpless, overgrown kid.

'My *father*?' I echo quietly but no one is listening. Colin likes it when we call him Dad.

There's a pot of coffee brewing. Colin always starts his day the same way: toast and coffee, unless it's a weekend in which case he has two lightly poached eggs, toast and coffee. I sling a tea bag into a cup as I refuse to drink coffee (it's loaded with chemicals) and click on the kettle.

'Make us another.' David thrusts his empty mug at me, spitting toast crumbs across the table.

I find myself pondering the possibility that my *real* brother has been kidnapped by aliens in the last couple of years and replaced with this extraterrestrial baboon.

'Won't you be late for work?'

'Naa, not really. I'll just blame it on the buses anyway.'

David doesn't worry about anything any more. He's so laid-back I'm surprised he can keep his lungs going in and out.

'There you go.' Mum puts his sandwiches down in front of him, all trussed up with cling film.

'I'm sure David could make his own sandwiches.'

'It's no bother,' replies Mum distantly as Colin clomps about upstairs. 'David!' she shrieks in exasperation as my brother takes the last of Col's toast.

'Bri's got more on the go.'

'Briony, watch the toast, you know Colin doesn't like it black,' she snaps at me as I rescue the pieces from the grill.

'Why don't you ever do anything to help?' I take my frustration out on my brother, but he just pulls a face.

'You know how things are,' I hiss, giving him that look, the look that says 'you know what I'm talking about', but he just bounces it straight back at me.

'Let's try to get off to a peaceful start this morning,' Mum pleads desperately, rearranging Colin's slices of toast. Colin needs to have everything *just so*. His toast has to be propped up to 'facilitate cooling' and to prevent it from getting soggy. We used to have a toast rack until it got swept off the table during a breakfast row. You'd think with all the money Colin's got he'd have bought himself a new one by now.

'What about my tea?' David whines as soon as he realises I haven't made him a second cup. He shoves his mug in Mum's face. 'I'm gonna be late.'

'Don't treat Mum like your personal slave.'

'It's okay, Bri, love.' She fills the kettle back up.

'No, it's not. Don't let him treat you like...'

But I can't say it. Colin is coming down the stairs. I let it go because this isn't the time or the place and, besides, I know it won't change anything.

The sun is out and warming the air as I walk to school and it feels more like spring than mid-September. I take this as a sign that things are getting better. I'm always looking for signs that things are getting better, something to take away the blackness that sits on my shoulders, day in, day out.

Still, today is going to be a good day, I can feel it. And if I can get to the other side of North Bridge Road before the traffic lights change, then it'll be a doubly good day. I like to set myself secret tasks like that, inventing meaningless good luck charms. The traffic lights change once I'm clear of the road and I head down Moston Street towards Fairfax Court School which beckons behind distant trees.

'Major news,' Francine hisses over trigonometry. 'Has Aysha told you? Karaoke, Friday night. Be there or be a two-dimensional figure with four sides of equal length, and four right angles.'

'What?'

'A two-dimensional, oh, forget it, a *square*.'

That's typical of Francine. She can't say things normally like the rest of us — she has to be different. Both her and Aysha are a bit like that. They need to be noticed.

'Karaoke? Where?'

'It's a private party.' Aysha leans across, keeping a watchful eye on Mr Jackson, our maths teacher. 'My sister goes to the gym, right? And the receptionist there is leaving, she's got a job on a cruise ship, singing or something.'

'Aysha, Aysha, Aysha,' interrupts Mr Jackson, with a

heavy sigh. 'While you may feel that you don't need to pay attention to the finer points of trigonometry with that undoubtedly superior brain of yours, others may wish to grasp just a little of the knowledge that it is my sad duty to impart, so at least give the rest of the class a chance to learn.'

Some people snigger.

'What did he say?' Lisa boggles her eyes at me.

Aysha recoils, watching Mr Jackson steadily.

'Anyway,' Aysha resumes after a suitable pause, 'I've scored us some tickets. My sister's cool about it anyway. It should be excellent.'

'I am the *queen* of karaoke,' Francine informs us.

'Will there be any decent lads there?' asks Lisa, with her one-track mind.

'Plenty. All the guys from the gym. Big guys. Big muscles.'

Lisa is positively drooling.

'You'll come, right?' Aysha asks.

Lisa nods enthusiastically. Aysha's eyes flick over to me. Suddenly the lightness inside me starts to fade.

'I don't know. It's hard for me to get out these days, what with mocks and everything.'

'We've got *weeks* before exams start.'

'You *never* come out any more,' Francine moans.

'Well, you know, my parents are kind of strict.'

'They can't be that bad. It's the weekend. What harm can it do?'

'Yeah but...' My heart sinks, swallowed up by the blackness once more. 'I'll see.' And I can see in their faces that they know the answer as well as I do.

I turn my attention back to trigonometry, try to lose myself in its angles. I can't explain to them the way things are right now – I'm not sure I really understand myself. I blame not going out on my parents being strict but it's not that simple. What if I went out and Mum and Colin really got into one? Who would be there to stop something really bad from happening? David doesn't care any more. I know Mum says she doesn't need or want my help but I feel I have to hang round anyway, just in case.

I wonder what Aysha and Francine and Lisa would say if I told them. Mum says everyone has ups and downs, so maybe they'd think it's normal. Maybe it's just me, making excuses because I'm not the same as everybody else. I always have this feeling of being out of step with the world. Perhaps it's down to that odd jigsaw piece I have inside me, the piece my *real* father left behind.

The squeaking of Mr Jackson's marker over the whiteboard and Lisa's whispering voice cut back into my thoughts. She's telling Francine and Aysha about developments with Steven Williams. Boys are all they seem to talk about these days. I want to be the same as them, think the same as them, but I can't shake the feeling that it's all so hopeless. You leave so much of yourself hanging in the breeze, exposed and open, when you get into a relationship. And that can't be a good thing, can it? Besides, I know how things end up.

Five

Weekends are the worst. Two days of bumping off each other in the house is enough to drive any family to distraction, right? And our family is no exception.

Mum and Colin have been bickering with each other since yesterday over Mum's sister Cath. She wants to invite Cath over for coffee but Colin's making a big song and dance about it.

'You knew I had plans for this weekend,' he grunts into the TV on Saturday night.

'It's just I haven't seen Cath for over a year now, and what with Hannah being away...'

'She's a troublemaker.'

'Who, Cath? She's my sister.'

'I don't want her coming to the house. I've got the garden to do. I told you that.'

'Well, perhaps she could take Briony out somewhere. Then she wouldn't be in the way and I would still get to see her. You'd like that, Briony, wouldn't you, love?' Mum shoots me a desperate smile.

'Aunty Cath? Yeah, sure. When's she coming?' I crack a smile.

'It would have to be next week now.'

'Yeah, we could go to the Winterbourne complex. She

won't have seen it.' I try to clear the atmosphere with a joke. 'Maybe I can get her to buy me a belated birthday present, what d'you think?'

Colin glowers in my direction.

'Oh, so I suppose now you think I don't provide for you well enough. Is that it?'

'No, I just meant – '

'Have you any idea how much it costs to keep you in that school of yours? And for what? To end up like that good-for-nothing brother of yours?'

David blushes and chews his nails. Mum opens her mouth to object but Colin scowls at her. It's unusual for Mum to be so persistent once Colin has made his feelings clear and I feel myself brace, waiting for the storm. But Colin marches out of the house, slamming the front door loudly behind him.

Today there's a tension in the house that makes it difficult to breathe, as if someone is slowly sucking out all the air. I find myself taking deeper and deeper breaths to get enough oxygen into my lungs. I pull on my trainers, desperate to be outside and on my own.

'Briony!' Mum appears from the kitchen in her pink Marigolds. 'You haven't forgotten it's Sunday?'

'How could I?'

'Well, I could use some help, you know.'

'So, ask David.'

It's a low blow but sometimes I want to lash out: I mean, why does she always have to dump on me?

'I've so much to do today.' She's speaking more to herself now. 'And I was going to make a quick dash to the supermarket as well.'

'Mum! I'm just going for a run. I'll be home in plenty of time. And the sooner you let me go, the sooner I'll be back.'

She looks shocked momentarily, then nods.

'Yes, sorry. Sorry, love.'

I make for the door.

'And stop being sorry all the time.'

But of course she doesn't hear me.

Sunday. The Lord's day. Ha ha. I sprint for the park. A day for families. Ha ha ha. I follow the line of the river. A day to get together with loved ones and pretend that all is well with the world. Ha bloody ha.

The muscles in the backs of my thighs are pulled tight because I never warm up the way we're told to at school. I do a lap of the park then head along the main road to the station. I want to forget about everything except the grey slabs of pavement disappearing under my feet, but I can't switch off. I can't turn my back on Mum however mad she makes me for putting up with Colin's continual crap. Sometimes I feel like shaking her. Not that it will do any good. *He* shakes her so violently sometimes that I think her head will snap right off her neck.

I turn at the next corner and head for home, my pace slowing the nearer I get. My senses become super-sharp as I slink through the back door, listening for clues, scanning the lay of the land. Colin is in the lounge reading the *Sunday Times*. I go upstairs and change my clothes. What a picture of middle-class *bliss* we must appear. The *Sunday Times*. Private school. Neat lawn. Clean house. So bloody respectable. Not the kind of family you would suspect for a moment.

Mum looks nervy when I go into the kitchen to lend her a hand, but then she always looks like that these days.

'Lay the table, Briony, love,' she whispers, adjusting the gas flame under the pots. 'Use the good napkins, and put a cloth out.'

Obediently I go into the dining room and pull out the matching linen tablecloth and napkins. We always have linen on Sundays – Colin likes it that way. I peek through the crack in the door at him. He's drinking whisky. It makes the muscles in my stomach wrench. Whisky is always a bad sign.

David appears in the doorway making a half-arsed attempt to match buttons with buttonholes on his shirt.

'What's for lunch?' He leans against the door jamb, watching me.

'How should I know?'

'What's up with you?'

'Nothing. What's up with you?'

'Eh?' He scratches himself. 'Where's Col?' His voice drops a little.

I motion towards the sitting room.

'Why don't you see if Mum needs a hand?'

David smirks. 'Thought that was your job.'

'Only because you're too bloody lazy to do anything.' I push the cutlery into his chest and shove past him. 'It wouldn't kill you to try to make things easier on her, you know.'

David sucks at his teeth.

'She brings it on herself, Bri.'

And right then and there I hate him, *really* hate him. Because I know that he's right.

On the wall of the dining room there is a portrait of 'the family' as we were when Mum and Col first got together. A friend of Colin's did it as a wedding present from a photograph of us all. I've never liked it. For one thing, the friend wasn't as good at painting as he thought he was and for another there's something eerie about having those empty faces staring blankly off the wall each Sunday as we eat lunch. But my dear stepfather is oddly attached to it for some reason. Perhaps it reminds him of the perfect family he once believed we were.

Mum places the dishes of vegetables in the centre of the table, double-checking everything. She looks frazzled.

'Lunch is ready, love.'

There is no movement from the other room. She hovers anxiously, unable to sit down until Colin is at the table. She disappears back into the kitchen, reappearing with salt and pepper. By this time Col has made his move and broods over the table staring testily into his whisky tumbler.

Mum vanishes back into the kitchen to get the plates which are warming on the hob. I stay where I am. Like I said, I don't see why it always has to be me who helps her. This *is* the twenty-first century, you know.

'How much longer do you intend fannying about in that kitchen, woman? A man could starve to death in here.' Colin calls in a tone somewhere between humour and irritation.

Mum brings the plates through, and Colin watches her closely with slightly drunken, clouded eyes. Deep down in the pit of my stomach I've got a bad feeling.

'What's this?' he demands pointing at his plate.

We are having gammon steaks with pineapple, except Col doesn't like pineapple so his steaks have two fried eggs on top of them.

'It's gammon.' says Mum, her eyes flicking nervously over to his plate.

'It's Sunday, Miriam.' His voice is almost sing-song. 'On Sundays we a have roast. Where's the meat?'

'Gammon's meat,' Mum squeaks.

I want to take a giant breath of air because I feel like I'm suffocating, but I'm paralysed and can't move.

'Gammon's meat,' echoes Colin, laughing to himself.

'Well, it's from a pig,' Mum flounders.

'You get *bacon* from a pig,' says Colin, holding the anger in check for just a moment longer. 'And bacon's for BLOODY BREAKFAST.'

We all jump. I quickly gasp for breath.

'There wasn't anything else that looked nice down the market.' Mum explains hastily. 'I was going to go again today but I never had time.'

'You stupid woman. All you've got to do in your bloody stupid life is go shopping and put food on the table and you can't even get that right, can you?' Colin puts his knife and fork down on either side of his plate. He seems calm again but this is how it is, up and down, calm then angry, angry then calm, like a cat playing with a mouse. 'I suppose you'd like me to do the shopping for you as well, would you, help you get it right, eh?' His voice is rising now. 'Well, I'm sorry that I can't, sorry that I can't do your job as well as my own, sorry that you expect me to do everything around here, sorry that you expect me to eat this SHIT.' And with that he snaps. He picks up the plate and hurls it at my mother. The gammon steaks are propelled through the air. One lodges itself behind the frame of our family portrait. The two eggs splatter ludicrously onto the faces of the canvas turning us into egg-headed aliens. I have to bite my hand to stop myself from laughing hysterically as yellow egg yolk slides down my stepfather's noble chin.

Colin's breathing is heavy and laboured, like a bull, fuelled with whisky and the bad news in the Sunday papers.

'I . . . I can make you something else.' Mum gets shakily to her feet.

Colin is already lumbering round the table to stop her. He grabs her by the throat, fingers digging in at either side of her neck, pulling her on to her tiptoes. She coughs, unable to breathe.

'Not good enough, Miriam!'

She raises her hands to his, attempting to pry away his fingers. He takes one hand off and slaps her hard, and she falls back into her seat. I want to scream, to grab him, but I am terrified and my legs have turned to stone.

'You want your sister to see you like this?' he barks, slapping her again.

So that's what this is all about. I should have guessed he wouldn't let it go.

Mum's eyes are wild and round. They scream out at me but all she says is: 'Briony, David, go to your rooms.'

David glances at me, momentarily unsure, as if I can tell him what he should do.

'That's right, get the sodding kids involved.' Colin grabs a handful of her hair in his fist and slams Mum's head down onto the table. When he draws it back there is blood on her face.

'Colin, please —' she whimpers.

'Please what? Please don't? You're right, Miriam. I shouldn't have to do this. You should bloody know by now but when are you going to learn, eh? When are you going to get it right? How many times do I have to bloody show you?'

I can see that Mum is dazed from having her head slammed into the table and I'm scared that if I don't do something, he might actually knock her unconscious.

'Dad – ' I start, though I have no idea what to say next.

He glances over his shoulder at me and then snarls back at Mum. 'Oh, that's it, is it? That's your game.'

'I . . . I don't know what you mean.'

'Turn the kids against me while you're at it, why don't you? D'you think I don't know what you're doing?'

He backhands her again with a clenched fist and the force of it topples her over. She hits the floor and scrambles away on all fours like an animal. Then Colin turns back to me and David.

'Bloody piss off.' He waves a drunken arm at us, catching a glass of water in the process. 'Sod off before I do the lot of you.'

I back towards the door, afraid to turn away from him in case he comes after me too. But he's calm now, reaching for his whisky tumbler. He settles back into his seat as if nothing has happened and wipes a hand over his face.

Outside I falter, listening to check that it really is over. Nothing. Silence. David looks at me. His face has gone hard. Then he turns and bolts for the front door, running out into the autumn sunshine. The glass at the top of the door rattles behind him as I go upstairs to the bathroom and puke up my breakfast.

Six

For a long time, I crouch in my bedroom straining to hear every little sound through the floor. Colin is still sitting in the dining room, probably supping at his whisky, while Mum comes and goes from the kitchen, clearing up around him. Eventually I hear him go to the garage and start up the car, even though he's been drinking all morning. The moment the sound of the engine fades into the distance Mum stumbles up to the bathroom to survey the damage to her face.

I tiptoe through the main bedroom to the gleaming en suite bathroom. In the middle of it, holding herself up against the basin is my mother. Beaten. Hurt. Broken. She jumps when she sees me, thinking, no doubt, that it must be Colin coming back to teach her another lesson. Then she slumps down onto the edge of the bath.

I run a facecloth under the cold tap and apply it gently to the swollen areas of her face.

'This can't go on, Mum.'

'I know, love.' She winces with the pain.

'So? When are you going to do something about it? I'm scared, Mum. One of these days he's *really* going to hurt you.'

It's ludicrous. She's hurt now, but over the months our

boundaries have changed. She knows what I mean when I say 'really hurt'.

'Briony, this is between me and your father. I don't want you getting involved.'

'But I'm already involved. Me and David both are. Whether you like it or not.'

'Briony – '

We both fall silent as a car drives past the house, but it's not Colin's.

'Mum, this is getting worse. *He's* getting worse, you have to see that. How much longer are you going to let him do this to you?'

'It's my problem, love.' She shakes her head sadly. 'I'll sort it out.'

'It's *not* your problem, Mum. It's *his*.' Tears of anger and frustration prick at my eyes. 'Why don't you just tell him that you're not going to put up with this any more?'

She puts her hands up to her forehead. 'It's not that easy, Bri. I make him angry sometimes, the silly things I do, and Colin's always been a bit quick tempered.'

'Come off it, Mum.' I have her by the shoulders and it's as much as I can do to stop myself from actually shaking her. 'This has got nothing to do with you making him mad. He's got a problem. And if you don't do something soon, God knows what he'll do next.'

I can't bring myself to say it, to tell her the thing I fear more than anything else. That one day he will actually kill her. I'm not saying that he'll intend to do it, just that one day when he's had one drink too many, he won't know when to stop. 'Sod off before I do the lot of you.' His words zing round my head like bullets. What does that mean?

'What can I do?' Mum's voice is barely audible.

She is so drained of life, she hardly seems to exist any more. It scares me because it forces me to acknowledge how bad things have become.

'You can always leave him, Mum.' I take her hands in mine and hold them tight.

Have I ever said this to her before? Maybe I've just thought it previously.

'Leave him, Mum. Before it's too late,' I say again, squeezing her hands to make her hear.

'Leave?' She looks at me as if I am out of my mind. 'Briony love, I can't just leave.'

'Why not?'

'You don't just leave someone because you're going through a bad patch. It'd destroy Colin if I did that.'

'Who bloody cares about Colin? He deserves it!' I almost shout. 'And this is way more than just a bad patch, Mum.'

'Briony, don't be so hard on him. Colin's a good man.'

'No he's not. He *hits* you.'

'That's just when he's angry. When he's had a bit to drink. He's not always like that, Bri, you know that. Remember the kind, loving man who took us in? Colin's still the same person underneath.'

'Is he?' I let go of her, swearing.

It's awful, but in that moment I think I come closest to understanding my monster of a stepfather. For a split second I am so frustrated that I really want to slap some sort of sense into her. Of course, I don't. That's the difference between me and Colin.

'He's a good man, Bri.' Mum looks up at me. 'You're too young to understand.'

'To understand what?' I gag. 'That he beats you? That

he calls you useless and stupid and makes out that you can't do anything right? What more is there to understand?'

'Plenty. You're just seeing the bad side.'

'Stop making excuses for him! You always make excuses.'

'I do not.' Her eyes well up with tears.

Now *I* have made my mother cry and her pain slices me in two. I drop to my knees and bury my head in her lap, sobbing. I hate myself for being unkind to her. I hate myself and I hate him and I hate absolutely everything and I cry because I don't think I can take much more of this.

'Whatever else Colin has done, he's never left us,' she whispers and strokes my hair and I cry all the harder because I just can't see how to get through to her.

Seven

'You missed a brilliant night on Friday.'

'Huh?'

'Friday. Karaoke. God, don't tell me you've forgotten already.'

Lisa slides off the desk and flops into a chair beside mine as Miss Parkinson, our form tutor, enters and gestures for her to get down.

'Oh no, no. I didn't forget.'

Friday night seems like a lifetime ago. I look at Lisa, wondering how she can think it's so important. Then I remember that I'm the one who's out of step with the rest of the world and of course these things are important. To everyone else.

'We did a Britney number, the three of us. Yeah, I know, don't say anything, but actually, it wasn't half bad. In fact, I'd say we were pretty awesome.'

She gives me a quick rendition. My face responds with a smile but I feel as though the rest of me is somewhere very far away.

'Aysha copped off with some guy from the gym. He must have been at least twenty. Ooh, but he was *fine*.'

'Lisa Stanley, are you and Briony Newman really determined to start the week off with a red slip?' Miss

Parkinson asks glancing up from the register.

Red slips are our school's way of keeping you in check. Three red slips and you get a week's detention and your parents are summoned to an interview with the head of year.

'Sorry, Miss P,' Lisa replies cheekily and our form tutor looks up again.

'Perhaps you'd like to collect your slip on the way out of registration.'

A ripple of subdued laughter goes round the room.

'Way to go, Stanley,' smiles Steven Williams, admiringly.

Lisa flushes. She doesn't give a toss for any red slip anyway.

On Mondays we finish the afternoon with IT, which is usually a good excuse to go to sleep or do some homework or something. Mrs Craft, our IT teacher, will often have a worksheet of tasks for us to complete, full of simple things like 'create a new file and save it to disk' or 'find X's address from the database'. We suspect that Mrs Craft is learning this stuff as she goes along whereas the rest of us have been doing it for years.

Nobody minds. When you finish you can play a game or go on the Internet. Francine and Aysha do nothing but sit there and text each other all lesson. Most teachers go mad if they see you playing with your phone during a lesson but the odd bleep of a text message is easily lost among the whir of the computers in the IT room. I share a computer with Aysha, and Lisa shares one with Francine, and because we sit at opposite ends of the room, there is a genuine need for the pair of them to send each other silly messages for an hour. I pretend to be interested. To be like everyone else.

We have finished our worksheet and Mrs Craft is

sitting behind the console at the head of the room, reading a gardening book. Francine approaches the desk clutching her stomach and moments later leaves the classroom. A minute or so afterwards, Aysha's phone emits three quiet notes followed by a fourth longer tone. She holds it under the desk and presses 'Read New Message'.

C U AT B BLCK LOOS IN 5 STHG 2 TELL U

Aysha waits a couple more minutes before asking if she can go to the toilet. Mrs Craft looks as if she knows something is going on but can't quite put the pieces together. Tiredly she nods and waves Aysha away.

I have nothing to do now. I am alone at a computer, sitting at the back of the room. I move the mouse over to the Internet icon, click on it and wait for the screen to change. We have a computer at home, of course – it's in the sitting room but I only use it for homework.

Presently the welcome screen flashes up in front of me along with the day's news headlines. Mrs Craft is still reading her book. I highlight the keyword box, and type in 'domestic violence', then press enter and wait. Probably whatever's there will be blocked by the school's password (which Steven reckons he's worked out). But then, surprisingly, a list of sites appears. I click on one, and the screen colours in slowly as it downloads.

I am excited, afraid. I scroll through the options. Domestic Violence Quiz: *Are You Being Abused?* Sexual Abuse: *Is Your Relationship Dangerous?* Marjorie Dawson answers YOUR Questions. The Secrets of Sexual Attraction. Love or Lust? Did You Know: *50 Little Known Facts About Abuse*. Understanding Your Mate. Interactive Chat, *speak to our psychologists and other women like yourself.*

Healing Message Board: *Post a Message Here.* The list goes on: Rape; My Shameful Secret; I Can't Take Any More; The Day He Almost Killed Me.

I scroll back and click on the Message Board. A box appears. It's full of people's questions and stories and the replies that they have been sent. I feel as though I am invading their secret world, spying on something private but I'm drawn in just the same and lean a little closer to the screen.

```
Subject: Leaving
From: Angel
I've been married for six years now
and in that time my husband has
verbally, emotionally and physically
abused me. For myself, I can take
it, but now we have a young son,
Martin. I don't think my husband
would ever lay a finger on him but I
don't want Martin to grow up in this
kind of environment. I know it's not
healthy but I'm scared to leave. I
so much want to get the strength to
take my life back but that's easier
said than done. I will lose so much
if I leave. And besides, if I was
going to do it, I should have done
it years ago. I just feel that it's
all too much for me.
```

I shiver as I read. There are hundreds of them. Hundreds just like Mum.

```
Subject: Re. Leaving
From: Lady-in-red
What will you lose if you leave him
except a life of violence and abuse
which is only going to get worse?

Subject: Re. Leaving
From: Legs11
If you fear your husband in any way
then you must get out. My mother was
killed by my father. She also believed
she could take it and that he would
never touch the kids. He did. I miss
my mother and I am still healing.
Don't wait. Be strong.
```

The classroom has faded away as I scroll through the answers to Angel's plight. Her words chill me to the bone. I want to know what's happened to her. The date on her message is just three days ago.

```
Subject: I can't take much more
From: Goldie
I have been married for 28 years and I
really think I will go mad if my
husband shouts at me one more time.
It's not always verbal. Sometimes he
beats me and locks me in the cupboard
under the stairs until I have 'learned
my lesson'. He makes me feel so small
and worthless. I am nearly fifty years
old and I feel that my life is over.
What am I to do?
```

A lump comes to my throat as I read Goldie's message. Twenty-eight years. Until I have learned my lesson. That's the language my stepfather uses. I picture a woman who is almost half-a-century old, someone's grandmother, cowering in the cupboard under her stairs. I look desperately for any replies to Goldie.

```
Subject: Re. I can't take much more
From: Girlfriend
It broke my heart to read your
message. You must be strong. You are
worth so much more, we all are. My
husband broke my arm before I plucked
up the courage to finally take myself
and my daughter out of that situation.
Life is so much richer once you are
out. Trust me. Look in the phone book
for places in your area that you can
go to. You can also ring your local
police station for details of shelters
and refuges. There IS help out there
if you want it. God bless you.

Subject: Depressed
From: Jim Carrey fan
Today I feel so depressed. Yesterday I
was going to go to a battered women's
meeting in my area but I couldn't
remember the address. So I phoned the
number and the girl tried to give me
directions but I was too scared to
write them down in case HE found the
piece of paper. I set off but I forgot
```

```
the house number and I walked up and
down for an hour crying and trying to
remember what she'd said. So I phoned
again but I got the answering machine
and there was nothing else for it but
to go home. I don't know. Maybe I
should have known I wouldn't do it.
I'm useless. He always tells me I'm
useless. Now I know he's right.
```

Aysha drops into the seat beside me and I nearly jump out of my skin. Clumsily I close the message board, but not before she's seen the rest of the screen.

'What's this? You found something hard core or what?' Her eyes have alighted on the sexual abuse heading. 'Is your relationship, what was that, dangerous?'

I close it down. Click on something unrelated.

'I like the sound of that.' She settles into her seat, shooting Mrs Craft a glance over the top of the computer. 'Dangerous men. Mmm. Did Lisa tell you about Friday?'

'The karaoke? Yeah.'

Aysha grabs the mouse off me and does a search for the word 'Sex'.

'About Robert,' she says into the screen, 'You should have seen him. Sex on legs. He was GORGEOUS.'

I don't want to hear about Robert's sexy legs or what Francine has just told her in the toilets or anything else. I just want to be out and running somewhere. Anywhere. I just know that I have to get out.

When I get home from school Mum is in the kitchen, spraying Mr Muscle over her surfaces. Dinner's in the oven, and there's no sign of David or Colin.

'I was on the Internet at school today,' I begin slowly, cautiously, trying not to get in her way.

Mum smiles, feigning interest.

'It was really good,' I continue nervously, not wanting to frighten her off. 'I got on to this one site and it was a kind of helpline for women.' I pause again. 'There were a lot of women talking about their experiences...' I hesitate. 'A lot of them are just like you.'

Mum's head jerks up sharply. She's suspicious.

'They're all in relationships where their partners have abused them in some way.' My heart is in my throat and I can't swallow.

'Briony! You haven't been talking about me to anyone, have you?'

'No. It's not like that. It's a message board. You can write messages and people send in their replies. I was just reading what other people were saying.'

'I mean it, Briony. I don't want you meddling.' She looks furious.

'I wasn't "meddling". Jesus.' I roll my eyes, Lisa-style. 'I just thought you might like to know that there are other people out there who know what you're going through.'

'What I'm going through?' Mum shrills. 'What I'm going through? What do you mean what I'm going through?' She drops a cup into the kitchen sink and scrubs at it furiously, keeping her back to me. 'What do you think you're trying to do to me, Briony, with all this nonsense you keep coming out with? I've got enough on my plate right now without having to deal with you as well.'

'I was only trying to help,' I explain.

'I don't need your help. I don't need anybody's help, thank you very much. The only thing I need right now is for you to stop stirring things up with Colin.'

'He hits you, Mum, in case you've forgotten,' I say sarcastically.

'You think married couples don't have arguments? Welcome to the real world, Briony. It's not all roses and candlelit meals, you know.'

'I know that,' I shout back. 'Don't make out like I don't know anything.' I hate it when she treats me like a stupid kid.

'Well, maybe when you get to my age you might see things a bit differently,' she sniffs.

'I bloody well hope not,' I snap and with that I stomp out of the kitchen and upstairs to my room.

Why does anyone put up with being treated so badly? I am out pounding the footpaths again, running like a thing possessed. The same questions keep revolving round and round in my mind. What is it that stops Mum from simply putting an end to Colin's reign of terror? Why can't the likes of Angel and Goldie and the Jim Carrey fan just get themselves out of there? Mum says it's not that easy, but isn't that just an excuse?

There's something I remember from our physics lesson today, really thrilling stuff on action and reaction. It goes:

'When two bodies collide, the force one exerts on the other is equal in size but opposite in direction to the force the second one exerts on the first.'

I think about this while I am running. Surely Colin can only bully Mum as much as she lets him? *Equal in size but opposite in direction*. If she stood up for herself, he wouldn't be able to do it. It's basic physics.

I stop to get my breath back. Above me the sky is alight with stars, always there, whichever way I turn, however far I run. I wonder what noise a star would make if you could get close enough to hear it. I like to imagine them as hollow wind chimes, echoing as the universe blows through them but I know in reality that they are giant, roaring balls of gas, a nuclear reaction that burns for billions of years before dying out. It's all just basic physics.

Eight

We're sitting in our personal and social development class. PSD is our school's preparation for the big bad world beyond the school gates. Today, with a week before the end of October and the start of half-term, the emphasis is on revision. Miss Kennedy is waffling on about how to use our free time constructively, ie study.

'For you this is not a holiday,' she warns. 'This is a chance to brush up on all those last minute bits of revision before the mocks. I'm assuming, of course, that you've already started revising.'

'Goes without saying really, don't it, Miss?' Steven pipes up.

'Forgive me if I don't share your confidence in your fellow classmates, Steven,' quips Miss Kennedy dryly.

Ian leans over to me. 'You'd think if they were so bothered about giving us time to revise, they'd knock these lessons on the head for starters. They are so boring.'

'Yeah, they are a bit.'

'And it's not like there's going to be an exam at the end of it, so what's the point?'

'I guess.' I catch Francine's eye across the room and she raises her eyebrows knowingly.

I wonder if Ian likes me. I wonder why he would like me.

'I've got a friend in another school and he says they don't start mocks till December.'

'Really?' My mouth is dry and I can't think of a thing to say.

'Yeah.' He sits back in his chair. Obviously I've bored him to bits already.

Francine is still watching me, and winks.

At lunch-time I don't go running, but head down to McDonald's with Lisa, Aysha and Francine. I feel like I need to spend some time with the old gang – so much has been slipping away from me lately.

'Thought you'd want to be out jogging this lunch-time,' Aysha comments.

The other two glance at her and I get the distinct feeling that they've been talking about me.

'Yeah well, you can't run all the time.'

Again they shoot furtive glances at each other, or maybe I'm just imagining it. Lisa blows the paper from her straw across the table at me.

'So what's the plan for half-term?'

'Remember I'm working on Saturday morning and Tuesday evening,' Francine reminds us.

'That still leaves us plenty of time,' Lisa says.

'You're not planning to do any revision then?'

'Maybe just a bit. Sunday night before we go back.'

'Yeah, that'd be right. Last-minute-Lisa,' Aysha laughs. 'And what about that bitch Parky giving us all that extra work to do?'

'I hate her,' Francine snarls. 'She really thinks she's something. Did you hear her yesterday? "If you coloured girls spent a little less time talking..." Coloured!' She rolls her eyes. 'I mean what colour does she think we are? Pink with purple spots?'

'Don't let her get to you. She's already given me one red slip this week,' Lisa says, playing with the packets of sugar.

'You always get red slips off her. She doesn't like anybody,' Aysha tuts. She stirs her mikshake with her straw. 'So, anyway, you think Steven Williams is going to pluck up the courage to ask you out before half-term?'

'*You* could ask *him* out,' Francine suggests.

'Yeah? And what if he says no?' Lisa pouts.

'He won't say no. He's been chatting you up for weeks now,' Aysha says confidently.

She's very sure of herself when it comes to the opposite sex. She's had more dates than the rest of us put together.

'What about Ian in PSD this morning?' Francine grins. 'I saw him leaning over and whispering in your ear.'

'It was only stuff about exams.' I feel like a rabbit caught in headlights.

'Doesn't matter. It's obvious he likes you.'

'To you maybe.'

'To anyone with eyes.'

'He's probably just doing it 'cos Steven is all over Lise.'

'Don't put yourself down all the time, Bri,' Francine retorts. 'I'll ask him if you like.'

My heart races. 'Don't you dare! Don't you dare say anything to him!'

They all look at me, sniggering.

'Don't worry, I'll be really subtle, you know, ever so casual.'

'You can't! Promise me you're not going to ask him.'

'Whatever.'

'Promise me!'

'I promise.' She laughs. 'Jesus! Loosen up a bit, Bri!'

All the way home, I can't stop thinking about Ian. What if he does ask me out? Suppose we go on a date and have nothing to talk about and the whole thing's a complete disaster? What if he asks about my family?

Tonight Colin has a big dinner with clients so I know he won't be home until late. He never asks Mum to accompany him to these things anymore – he says they wouldn't interest her, that she would be bored, and Mum just smiles and says 'whatever you think, love'. Colin always knows best.

Of course, the whole thing with the gammon steaks has never been mentioned. A few days later Colin claimed he'd landed a new contract at work and brought home wine and flowers for Mum – his attempt at an apology, I suppose. He's always like that. One minute he'll be raving like a mini-Hitler and the next he thinks he's Prince Charming. I wonder if everyone's relationships are like this.

I sit at the computer after dinner while Mum loses herself in some glossy magazines in the kitchen. As usual David is out with another part-time girlfriend. I log on to the Internet and search out the site I found at school a few weeks back. I don't really want to be drawn into these people's lives but I'm curious to know what's happened to Angel and Goldie and the depressed Jim Carrey fan. Among the entries, there are some replies to their original messages.

```
Subject: Re. Depressed
From: Silver Lady
You don't realise it now but you are
```

```
drained of energy. He is taking
everything from you because by keeping
you down, he can make sure you're not
able to fight back. Just talking to
someone who knows what it's like is the
first step. Call the helpline number
again and remember you're worth more
than this. May God be with you at all
times.

Subject: Re. Re. Depressed
From: Lady-in-Red
SL is right. It's hard to see it at the
time when you feel so tired, physically
and mentally. Take it from those who
have been there before you. My husband
took everything from me but most
importantly he stripped me of my self-
respect. And if you believe you are
worth nothing you can hardly find the
strength to get out of bed in the
morning, let alone change your life.
That's how they want you to be.
Remember that. Try to be strong.
```

I leave the message board and go on to the '50 Little Known Facts About Abuse'. Mum comes through to check the telly pages.

```
Fact 1: Women are six times more likely
to be attacked and physically harmed by
someone they've had a relationship with
than a stranger.
```

```
Fact 2: In the United States, a woman
is beaten every fifteen seconds.
Fact 3: Domestic violence is best
defined as emotional, psychological,
physical or sexual abuse that one
person uses over another for the
purposes of control. It ranges from
name calling through to potentially
lethal physical harm and/or assault.
```

'What are you doing, love? I don't want you on that computer all night.' Mum brushes past me.

'Just homework.' I lie.

'So long as you're not too late to bed. You've got exams soon. You need to get your sleep.'

She picks up a mug Colin has left down by his armchair, straightens a coaster and goes back to the kitchen. She lives every day as though there is absolutely nothing wrong. But somewhere deep inside, she *must* know things aren't right.

```
Fact 15: It is a myth that domestic
violence occurs only in poor urban
areas. Women of all cultures, races,
occupations, income levels and
geographic regions are battered.
```

At least Mum is in good company.

```
Fact 37: Many abusers attempt to
control the other partner by forbidding
them from seeing family or friends.
```

Now that sounds familiar. I move the mouse, scroll down further.

> Fact 50: Being a friend or relative of a victim of domestic violence is never easy. Many women feel they 'deserve the abuse' and often love their partners in spite of it. Trying to help someone with this mind set is difficult. First you must help the victim get to the point where they recognise that they need help.

That gives me an idea. If Mum won't phone Aunty Cath, then *I* will. If she just turns up out of the blue, then Colin won't be able to say anything, will he? And maybe seeing her again will encourage Mum to do something, or say something. One thing I'm sure of is that it will do her good to have someone to talk to for once, some contact with the outside world.

While Mum is upstairs faffing around in the bathroom, I get the phone and the black leather book that sits in the desk drawer, and quickly punch in Aunty Cath's number. I listen carefully for any sign of Mum coming down. It's important that she knows nothing about this or she'll only go and tell Colin.

The phone rings and rings and I will Aunty Cath to pick it up. Still no reply. I glance at my watch and realise she's probably out or in bed or something. Suddenly I hear Mum's footsteps on the stairs and I slam the receiver down, slipping the phone book back to its rightful place and scurrying into the kitchen. Maybe I'll find time to phone again tomorrow evening.

I go to bed early because I don't want to be downstairs when Colin comes back. I think about what I will say to Aunty Cath tomorrow – how I will get her to visit us without arousing suspicion. As I lie there I can see the blinking of the stars through the gap in my bedroom curtains and for once, sleep drifts in easily. For the first time in ages it feels as if I have the answers to the world in my hands.

Nine

Tonight my brother doesn't even bother making an appearance for dinner.

'Where's David?' I ask Mum. She sighs irritably at my question.

'That boy's got his own agenda these days.'

I feel a flash of anger towards him. He is growing more and more detached from everything that happens at home. Even though he's a selfish baboon, he could at least try to make some sort of effort.

'He treats this place more like a hotel sometimes,' mutters Mum.

'If you don't like what he's doing, why don't you say something? I mean, he's an adult now, isn't he? He should be pulling his weight.'

But as usual any criticism of my darling brother falls on deaf ears.

After dinner, Colin and I sit in the living room watching TV. There's not much on – just the usual collection of boring DIY programmes and variations on the vet theme, but anything's better than maths revision.

Suddenly the phone starts to ring. Colin reaches over and answers it.

'Hello? Cath! What a nice surprise.' He looks directly

at me as he speaks. My stomach is doing somersaults. 'Oh, really? I don't know... er, actually she can't come to the phone right now... yes, she's out... I couldn't tell you.' My insides are in knots. 'Certainly will. Yes. Okay. Will do. You take care now.'

As he replaces the receiver his whole face has changed. He gets steadily to his feet and heads slowly towards the kitchen where Mum is busy doing the dishes. His eyes have a far away, fixed look to them. I want to scream out to Mum. *Run. Hide.* But of course no sound comes out of my mouth – I'm frozen.

'Miriam. You'll never guess who that was on the phone just now.'

Mum spins round at the sound of his sing-song voice. He's leaning in the kitchen doorway.

'It was Cath. Your sister.'

'Cath? I wonder what she wanted,' Mum smiles nervously, turning back to her washing-up.

'I was rather hoping you could tell me that.' Colin pushes himself off the door jamb.

Mum glances round, catching something in his voice. 'How should I know? I didn't speak to her.'

'It seems that when she got home last night she dialled 1471 and got our number. How d'you think that happened Miriam?'

'I... I don't know. I haven't spoken to her in ages.'

Colin shakes his head. 'You must think I'm a complete idiot. Going behind my back like that, thinking I wouldn't find out.'

'Colin, I really don't know what you're talking about.'

'Like hell you don't!'

My legs feel like pillars of concrete as I stumble to the kitchen table.

'It was me. I phoned Aunty Cath.'

For a moment they both just stare at me. Okay, I can take whatever's coming, I think, just leave Mum alone for once.

'*I* phoned her. Yesterday.'

Colin's face is like thunder. Clearly this was not part of his plan. Mum shuffles sideways, away from him. Eventually he says to me: 'Get out of here. This has nothing to do with you.'

I take a gulp of air. It seems cold against the back of my throat. 'But I was the one who phoned her.'

But Colin doesn't seem to hear me. He turns back to my mother. 'So you've got this little whore covering for you now. Very clever. Very clever indeed.'

'What she says is true, Col, love.' Mum flinches. 'I don't know anything about that phone call.'

'You lying little slag.' He grabs her by the arm.

'No, really. I swear.'

'Leave her alone. It was *me* that made the call,' I squeak.

Colin puts his hand at the back of Mum's neck, clasping a handful of hair. He pulls her and himself towards me.

Suddenly I can't take it any more. Mum won't look at me. I turn and fly out the back door, tears streaming down my face. I stand out in the pitch black of the garden and sob.

When I come in again, the house is quiet. I find Mum kneeling on the lounge floor, her face in her hands, and she's crying like a little child. I feel sick, and guilty for leaving her.

'Mum, are you okay?'

My mother drops her hands from her face, which is white under smeared streaks of blood. The phone lies in pieces on the floor, the cord ripped right out of the socket. I reach out to help her up but she just sinks back down on her heels and stares at me.

'Just leave me alone, Briony. For God's sake, leave me alone,' she whispers.

'Mum?' I feel hollow.

'What are you trying to do to me? Haven't you done enough harm already?' She hauls herself painfully to her feet.

'I didn't know Aunty Cath would call back. I didn't think.'

'Didn't think?' She looks at me with contempt. 'You thought plenty. You've never liked Colin, you've always wanted us to break up, haven't you? Haven't you?!'

'Mum, no!'

She drops her eyes to the floor and the broken phone.

'Get out of my sight, Briony. I can't deal with you right now. Just go.'

I lie awake listening to the sounds from the street. Tonight my mind refuses to shut down. I'm desperate for sleep but still it refuses to come. All I can think is: Mum hates me, hates me for trying to help. Meddling she calls it. Trying to break her and my stepfather up. I feel guilty because it's true. I would love them to split up. Leave Colin high and dry in his fancy house with all its nice things to polish and clean and keep *just so*. Maybe if he did a bit more around here he'd realise how hard my mother works all day every day, instead of telling her she's let herself go, she doesn't look nice any more, her cooking is shit.

It doesn't matter though. Mum hates me. Loves Colin. I don't understand anything anymore. I wish I was more like David. Wish I could just switch off my thoughts, my feelings, my whole self. Wish Mum had never met Colin. Wish my father was still here. But then, how can I wish for that? He must have done something really awful to just leave us the way he did. Which makes him a really terrible person. And I must be just like him. Just ask my mother.

Ten

When the alarm rings at seven, I wake feeling heavy and leaden. As I stagger to the bathroom, it feels as though I am walking through water. My eyes are hot and gritty, red with lack of sleep. I wonder what Mum will look like this morning, what lies she will invent to cover the bruises that can't be disguised with make-up and long sleeves.

When I drag myself through to the kitchen I am greeted by a peculiar sight. Colin is beavering away, putting boiled eggs and toast on a tray. David is hunched over a bowl of cereal, saying nothing.

'As I explained to your brother here, you two will have to fend for yourselves this morning,' he announces casually. 'Your Mum's feeling a bit tired so she's having breakfast in bed and a bit of a lie in.'

He takes a small vase with flowers in it from the window sill and sets it next to the toast, then whisks the tray off the table and takes it upstairs to Mum. It's as if yesterday never happened.

He makes me feel sick.

I'm tempted to keep walking along Moston Street, just keep going straight on and not turn into the school gates. Not sure that I can face it today. Not sure that I can keep putting on this brave face, making out like nothing's wrong. It's hard to be two different people the whole time. But Miss Kennedy is on duty and sees me before I have a chance to escape.

I will be all right as long as no one speaks to me, I think. But no such luck. Lisa catches me at the lockers and she's brimming with something.

'Okay, today's the day. I can feel it,' she says, leaning against the wall. 'Steven's going to ask me out, for sure.'

I close my locker and she straightens up.

'Okay, I know, I can't be sure but I've just got this feeling. I mean, there's no law that says I can't make the first move or anything, but I think he's going to say something. God, what's the matter with you? You look like shit.'

I shake my head as the bell grinds out the time. Five minutes to get to our form rooms. We duck into the loos.

'Are you sick?' Lisa stands behind me as I grip the basin and look at myself in the mirror. 'Or are you just in one of your moods again?'

I look up at her. 'I am *not* moody.'

'You are so. You're one of the moodiest people I know.'

This attack throws me, and for a moment I can think of nothing else except proving that she's wrong.

'Why am I moody?'

'I don't know. You tell me. You never used to be like this.' She examines her teeth in the mirror, checking for bits of breakfast, then glances back at me obviously waiting for some kind of explanation.

'Yeah, well, right now I just hate my life, okay?' I look at my mouth, speaking the words. 'I really, really hate my life.'

The moment hangs in the air for a split second, then Lisa nods, rolls her eyes the way she does, and exclaims:

'God, tell me about it.' She clearly thinks this is just another case of teenage angst.

I am off the hook and give her a tired smile. It takes all my energy to make my mouth curl up like that.

'Yeah, I know what you mean. Sometimes I hate mine too. Everything. My hair, the way I look, my parents, our house. Especially my parents. Sometimes, God...' she tosses her head back, 'sometimes I just hate everything. It's all so... aghh, boring, I guess. That's why something definitely has to happen with Steven today, otherwise I swear I'm going to go mad.' She pauses for breath, then glances at me. 'We should be going. Come on, cheer up, after tomorrow it's half-term. Just think about Ian and you'll feel loads better.'

I wish my life was that simple.

On the last Friday before half-term Steven Williams finally makes his move. It happens in the lunch room. He and Ian sidle over to sit with me and Lisa and I realise that Francine and Aysha are nowhere to be seen, which is unusual. Then it all starts to make sense.

'So, you all prepared for mocks?' he asks.

Lisa shrugs. 'As much as possible. What about you, Bri?'

I look up. 'Me? Yeah, well, I've done some. I guess I'll use half-term to do some more.'

'Yeah, suppose we should too.' Steven looks at Ian.

'Can't study all the time though, can you?' Ian shrugs.

'Remember what Miss Kennedy said,' Lisa offers. 'Break it down into – '

'Manageable chunks,' they all chorus, then laugh.

I don't feel a part of things but Lisa keeps looking over at me, trying to include me. I know what she's doing.

'God, I'll be glad when it's all over.'

'What next year?'

'Yeah. Next summer. Next summer is going to be excellent. Nothing to do, no homework, no coursework, nothing.'

We try to imagine what this will be like. I find it hard to imagine anything beyond the here and now.

'We'll have to have a HUGE party,' says Steven.

'Too right. We can burn all our books,' Ian grins.

'Count us in, eh, Bri?' Lisa raises her eyebrows.

I manage to smile back.

'Anyway, we've still got to get through mocks first.'

'Yeah, don't remind me. I wish I could wake up tomorrow and it'd all be over.'

I'm busy tracing patterns across my plate with my finger, not really listening.

'You know,' Steven says casually, 'we should arrange to do something, the four of us, in the middle of the week or something, so we've all got an excuse to stop revising.'

'Yeah,' agree Lisa and Ian, as if this idea has just come straight off the top of his head.

'There's a bonfire party on the common on Friday, I think.'

'Yeah, and we could go somewhere like Wolfie's,' suggests Ian. 'I hear it's really good. The drinks are cheaper midweek. What d'you think?'

There is more agreement. Lisa says it'll be good to have something to look forward to.

'Won't it, Bri?' she prods.

I nod. Smile (or grimace). Right now I think I'd agree to anything.

Ian and Steven stay a couple more minutes. Steven takes Lisa's number so that they can arrange something, then the boys take their trays back to the counter and disappear out into the corridor. Lisa turns to me.

'Jesus, you couldn't have made that any harder if you'd tried, could you?'

'What?'

She pulls a face. 'You! You sit there like you're sucking a lemon and hardly say one word. What's Ian going to think?'

'To be honest I don't really care what he thinks,' I reply moodily.

'Yeah, well, that's bloody obvious. God, Briony, sometimes I don't know why I even bother being your friend. You make everything so... so difficult.'

And with that she takes her tray and storms off, no doubt to report back to Francine and Aysha on what a lousy best mate I am.

It's the afternoon now and it's pouring with rain. The sky is grey and thunderous. Mr Stevens is forced to break from his monologue on urban planning to flick on the lights. The classroom is suddenly bathed in yellow.

Lisa and I have hardly spoken three words to each other since lunch-time. I feel lost and exposed, as if I have been stripped of that other me, the mask that I carefully put on each day as I walk through the school gates.

Lisa said I was moody and it plays on my mind. Obviously I wasn't fooling anyone as much as I thought I was. She said she didn't even know why she was my friend.

A whirlpool of emotions churns away inside me. I feel angry. With myself. With Lisa. With my mother. With Colin. With life in general. My pen loops endless angry circles on the page. I am tired of being who I am.

Dear God, please kill me.

'Jesus, what's up with you?'

Lisa leans across and puts a line through the words I have just written among my geography notes.

'Don't put stuff like that,' she shudders. 'It's freaky. God, Bri, what's going on with you these days?'

I stare down at my note book. Lisa glances back to the board where Mr Stevens is writing something for us to copy down.

'Bri, talk to me. What's up?'

'Nothing,' I shrug. 'I told you already. My life's shit.'

'Yeah, but writing that, what you did...'

'Sometimes I just feel that way, okay?'

'No, *not* okay! Tell me why! What's wrong?'

I shrug my shoulders again. 'There's just stuff going on at home right now. My mum and my stepfather aren't getting along. They've been fighting, really fighting like you wouldn't believe.'

There I've said it. I feel dizzy at having spoken the words out loud. I look up to see what has changed, what is different now that I have told someone. But absolutely nothing has changed. It comes as a bit of a shock to realise that the whole world is not going to suddenly cave in on me just because I have spoken these words out loud.

'I just wish my mum would leave the bastard,' I whisper as Mr Stevens begins to drone on again in the background.

'It'll get better,' Lisa says gently. 'Every relationship has bad times, even your parents'. My mum and dad went through something similar last year. Dad even moved out for a week, but then he came back and they made up and Mum reckons it's better than ever now. Your folks'll get through it, Bri, somehow. Just give them some space to sort themselves out.'

I know Lisa means well but her words just make me want to cry. I feel like no one understands. Not even me.

Eleven

The house is quiet when I get home. I listen for any sounds then sneak up the stairs and knock softly at the bedroom door.

'Mum?'

There's no response so I push it open. Inside it's dark and the curtains are still drawn.

'Mum?'

She's lying in bed. She rolls over slowly as I approach.

'Mum? Are you all right?' I can hear the panic creeping into my voice.

'I'm fine, Briony love, really.'

'Why are you still in bed? Why are the curtains closed?'

'The light was hurting my eyes.'

I perch on the edge of her mattress. As my eyes become accustomed to the blackness I can see there's a dark line across the bridge of her nose and marks around her eyes.

'Mum, you're not all right.'

'I'm fine, Briony. Don't make such a big deal about it.'

'Big deal? I think he's broken your nose.'

'I don't want to hear it, Bri.'

'Mum, please!'

She looks at me. Her voice is suddenly serious and unwavering. 'He's apologised, Briony. We had a long talk and he's sorry. *Really* sorry. He's promised me that it's never going to happen again.'

'How can you believe him?'

'I *have to* believe him.'

'He's going to keep doing it, Mum, as long as you keep letting him.'

'No, Briony. Things are going to be different from now on,' she insists. 'Trust me. This time things will be better.'

'But he's said that before. You're even beginning to talk like him.'

'Briony, don't make things difficult for us. Colin means it this time.'

'How do you know?'

'Because I know him. And whatever else you may think, I know him better than you do.' Mum softens slightly. 'Look, if you really want to help, then you can make dinner tonight. I'm really not feeling up to cooking.'

I nod and a fat, hot tear plops onto my cheek.

'We'll have steak, it's Col's favourite, and David never says no to steak, does he? Get them out of the freezer and put them in the microwave to defrost.'

'Mum – '

'You can do chips. Whatever you fancy. And Briony, please, for me, just try to be nice to your stepfather. I can't take the pair of you at each other's throats the whole time.'

I am helpless to do anything more.

For Mum's sake, I defrost four big steaks and peel potatoes and chip them and put some frozen peas in salt water, doing it all automatically, just going through the motions so that I don't have to think any more. Switch off my brain. Switch off my feelings. I can do this, I tell myself.

Me, David and Colin sit in the kitchen and have dinner while Mum has hers on a tray in her room.

'We're all going to have to pitch in and help a bit more till your mum's feeling better,' says Colin.

I think he truly believes she's ill.

'We can start with the dishes. I'll do them if you unpack the washing machine, Briony.' He smiles at me. 'And perhaps The Boy David here'll give us a hand putting things away.' He turns to my brother. 'What d'you say?'

David shrugs. 'Yeah, whatever.'

'Good.' Colin beams. 'That's sorted then.'

He is so upbeat that I want to laugh out loud. But if I start laughing, I might not be able to stop.

'So what's happening at school these days? Your mum says you've got exams soon.'

I stare at him for a couple of moments, unable to get my head round this whole happy-family-meal thing.

'Mocks. After half-term.'

'Of course, it's half-term, isn't it? I forgot. Well, just make sure you do some revision and don't spend all day watching TV.'

'I won't,' I sigh, then add, 'although, some friends have invited me out one evening next week, you know, as a break from studying.'

I look at him. I'm not exactly asking for his permission but...

'Good idea,' he nods. 'All work and no play makes Jill a dull girl, right? Just make sure you're back at a reasonable hour. Don't want you going down with this bug right before your exams, now, do we?'

I shake my head. No, we don't want that at all.

Twelve

Steven has arranged with Lisa that the four of us will meet up on Wednesday evening. She drops by one morning to tell me, complaining that she can't get through on our phone. I feign ignorance as to why it no longer works. Her mother is taking her shopping so she can't stay, she tells me, leaving me standing on the doorstep with my love life signed, sealed and delivered: a date, a foursome. I wonder why I don't feel as happy about it as I should.

Instead I try to concentrate on the fact that I've scored one over on Colin. I know there's no way he's going to say anything after what happened last week. Mum re-emerged from her room on Saturday afternoon, heavily made up, trying to cover the purple blotches around her eyes. I can still see the bump on her nose but I try not to look too hard. If we don't talk about it, maybe it will all go away.

On Wednesday, I pack some clothes into a bag and head over to Lisa's place a good two hours before we're supposed to be meeting Steven and Ian. Lisa's going to do my make-up. We sit in her room with a CD blaring and experiment with colours.

'I wonder what they're gonna wear. You think they'll bother to dress up?'

'I don't think they'll be in their school uniforms, if that's what you mean.'

'D'you think Steven's the hairy chest type?'

I shudder.

'Maybe not. Oh, well, try this.' Lisa thrusts an eye shadow at me.

I smudge it over my eyelids and look at myself in the mirror. My face stares solemnly back at me. I hate my freckles.

'Cheer up, you look more like you're going to a funeral.'

'I just don't know what the big deal is.'

Lisa opens her mouth to come back with something, then stops herself.

'Look, you'll have a good time, I know you will,' she smiles kindly. 'You're still worried about your mum, aren't you?'

I nod.

'Don't worry, I promise it won't always be like this. Things have a knack of sorting themselves out, one way or another. It gets better, Bri. Take it from someone who's been there.' She smiles and I look into her face to see whether or not it's true.

Two hours later we emerge from the house and head towards the Winterbourne complex where we've arranged to meet the boys. I feel self-conscious with my painted lips and eyes but Lisa sparkles.

'You don't think we've overdone things? What are they gonna think?'

'I told you, we're heading to Wolfie's afterwards. You don't want to be sitting there looking like you've just come off a farm or something.'

'Thanks a lot.'

'You know what I mean. The natural look is all very

well but sometimes you just need to dress up a bit, make more of an effort, you know.'

'Maybe I'm happy the way I am,' I say, trying not to hear how sad I sound.

'God, that's not them is it? They're early.'

I glance at my watch. 'We're late, you mean.'

'Yeah, well, good. Don't want to appear too eager, do we?'

Lisa grabs my arm and tugs me towards the other side of the shopping mall, out of sight.

'Come on. We'll sneak up on them from inside.'

I look at her, wondering what she's up to. 'Why? They're right there. We said King Street.'

'I know what we said, but it'll unnerve them. Take it from me. Never let them know what you're going to do next. Always keep them guessing.'

'I thought this was supposed to be a night out watching fireworks, not a war or something!'

Lisa nods gravely. 'Love, war. They're all the same when you get down to it.'

She's beginning to sound like Aysha – the voice of teenage experience.

Steven jumps as Lisa sneaks up behind him and covers his eyes with her hands. I stand there like a third leg as they laugh and joke around. Ian smiles at me and raises his eyebrows in a 'don't they go on a bit' sort of way. It all seems very strange considering we've only ever seen each other in a classroom before, and everyone knows school is nothing like real life.

'Are you okay about the fireworks?' Steven asks. 'I mean, it's only a small thing over at the FE college.'

'I thought there was a big display up on the common?' moans Lisa.

'That's Friday. Hey, we can go to that too if you want.'

'We'll see. Oh, well, come on then.' Lisa tosses back her shiny, black hair, links arms with me and marches us off ahead of the boys. They jump after us not noticing the sly smile Lisa flashes me. She's enjoying this.

The fireworks actually aren't that bad and there's a couple of food stalls selling things like jacket potatoes and burgers. We get hot dogs served with some transparent green sludge that we are led to believe is fried onions, then stand back and watch the display: me and Ian, Lisa and Steven.

'So what d'you think of my fake ID then?' Ian pulls his student card from his jeans and angles its shiny surface into the light.

'How did you get it?' I hold it in my hands.

I can stare long and hard at the photo whereas I definitely can't stare at him. Ian has dark hair and eyebrows. His mouth is wide, a bit like a frog's, but I kind of like that.

'Yeah, yeah, don't say anything about the picture, right?' He whisks it away from me and stuffs it back into his jeans. 'I was having a bad hair day.'

'Bad face day more like!' sniggers Lisa.

'So how did you get the ID?' I ask again.

'My brother works part-time at a printers. It was his idea actually.'

'Handy.'

'The trick is to memorise the year you were born, you know, the year you would have been born according to the card. That's what bouncers always try to catch you out with.' He suddenly looks sheepish. 'I'm not saying I spend all my time in pubs and clubs. Just occasionally. You know, with my brother.' He smiles, then looks at me. 'So, you got any brothers or sisters?'

I nod, tell him a little bit about David. 'But we're not that close,' I conclude.

And it's true, I realise, though it hasn't always been that way. A lot has changed over these last four years. I shiver, and turn my attention back to the fireworks.

When the display has finished and the smell of burning fills the air, we wander back into the centre of town, heading for Wolfie's. There's a bouncer in a black bomber jacket on the door but he's so deep in conversation on his mobile phone that he doesn't even notice the four of us sliding past him.

We sit in the darkest corner of the pub, far away from the bar staff, but we really don't look younger than anyone else here. Ian with his fake ID goes and gets the drinks while Steven, or Steve, as he now insists on being called, does his best to entertain Lisa and me. The two of them seem well matched, now that I think about it, a right pair of jokers. I can't imagine either of them taking life too seriously. Ian, on the other hand, is darker, deeper. You could probably go out with him for a whole month and still not know a thing about him.

He comes back armed with our drinks and sits on the stool next to me, shooting me a shy smile. I reach quickly for my drink, search my head for things to say. Lisa starts a conversation about football. I wish I had something to contribute but it's not a subject I know anything about. Presently Ian gets up again, this time to go to the loo. Moments later Steve follows after him. Lisa shakes her head, watching them go.

'I thought it was supposed to be us females who go to the toilet in pairs! What's Steve going to do? Hold it for him?' She looks at me. 'Are you okay? Not still thinking about stuff at home are you?'

I shrug.

'Just relax. Have another drink. This is dead easy to get down your neck anyway. It just tastes of strawberries.' She giggles and it occurs to me that she's already drunk. 'You can't taste the alcohol, at least not until you're out of your skull.' And she giggles some more.

I feel uncomfortable. Slightly dizzy, slightly sick. Maybe it was the hot dog. I wish I could take everything in my stride the way Lisa seems to. I reach for the bottle to steady myself. I can do this, I tell myself. I can be just like everyone else. Maybe if I drink this down a little quicker, I'll relax more.

'Here they come!' Lisa laughs as Steve and Ian amble back to our table.

'So, did you miss us?' Steve winks.

'Actually we weren't aiming for you, mate,' Lisa retorts coolly.

Steve shuffles his stool closer to Lisa's, dead casual. Ian straddles his and our knees brush together sending this weird electric shock up under my skin.

'So what sort of stuff are you into?' he asks me. 'What about music?'

We chat a bit about CDs and bands, keeping our voices low unlike Steve and Lisa who seem to be vying with each other to see who can be the loudest.

'Keep it down you two,' Ian mutters. 'D'you want us to be thrown out or what?'

Lisa waves away his concern then giggles as the bouncer walks past us on the way to the toilets. When he comes back she winks at him.

'What?' she says as we all stare at her. 'Come on, he's not going to expect someone who's under-age to do that, is he? It's all very well keeping a low profile but sometimes you've just got to front it out a bit.'

'She's mad.' Ian turns back to me, shaking his head.

'Tell me about it.'

'You know, you two don't seem like you should be best friends. You're so different.'

I stiffen, gulp at my drink. 'You mean I'm boring?'

'No, I never said that. You're very touchy, aren't you? I just meant you're quieter than her.'

I shrug my shoulders, pray for divine inspiration in the conversation department.

'And it wasn't meant in a bad way,' he assures me. 'It makes you more, I don't know, well, more interesting, I guess.'

I try and look nonchalant at this unexpected compliment, sip frantically from my bottle in an attempt to play it cool, and hunt desperately for something witty and *interesting* to say.

'Anyway, you're quieter than motormouth over there,' I tell him, nodding towards Steve.

'Hey, I heard that,' he grunts.

Lisa smiles at me. 'Watch out, Briony's getting into her stride. You don't know what she can be like sometimes.'

I think she's pleased I'm finally loosening up a bit. Strawberry alcohol tingles through my veins.

Ian shakes his head. 'What are the two of them like, eh? Maybe we should go out without them one day, you know, just to get some peace,' and he laughs awkwardly, catching my eye.

I laugh back, then suddenly realise he's trying to ask me out and my heart leaps into my mouth. He raises his eyebrows in a question.

'Yeah, whatever.' I laugh nervously. 'We'll probably not be able to think of anything to say to each other though.'

'Yeah, well, sometimes you don't need to say anything to have a good time. Most people go on too much about stuff that isn't really important.'

He smiles at me with his wide, froggy mouth and instantly I begin to relax.

By the time we are ready to leave the pub, Lisa and Steve are holding hands. I feel very conscious of this, mainly because Ian and I are *not* holding hands. We say goodbye outside the Winterbourne complex but not before Steve drags Lisa off to a doorway for a bit of serious face sucking. Ian and I stand there, awkwardly, waiting for them.

'I meant what I said about the two of us going out on our own some time,' he says.

'I know.'

'So you'd be up for it?'

'Sure, why not? I had a good time tonight.'

'Me too. You know, I'd write down your phone number but I haven't got a pen.'

'Me neither. I guess it'll have to wait till we're back at school then.'

He nods. Smiles. Steve ambles back towards us, calling out to him. Ian leans over and gives me a peck on the cheek, winks goodbye, then the pair of them head off together.

I have a funny feeling inside me. Reckon it might be the alcohol.

Wouldn't it be great if you could bottle your emotions like a perfume? I would squeeze all these good feelings I have right now into a container and then, when things aren't as good, I could ease out the stopper, take a good long sniff and instantly be transported back to this moment.

Thirteen

I wake up early on Monday morning then realise I don't have to get out of bed just yet. The mocks begin today. My first exam is physics and it doesn't start until half past nine. My stomach fizzes with nerves.

As I walk to school I have two main thoughts: one, I haven't done enough revision, and two, I'll be seeing Ian for the first time since last Wednesday. He doesn't do physics but I'm sure I'll run into him some time today. It feels good to have something normal to worry about. Mum and Colin seem to be bumping along quite nicely at the moment. Maybe we've all turned a corner, I think, as I turn down Moston Street, beating the traffic lights and my own secret deadlines. Maybe Mum's right. Maybe things have changed. Maybe everything is going to be okay.

In the exam room I line up all my pens and pencils so that they point in the same direction. Physics. The laws of attraction, force, movement and energy. I take a deep breath and turn over the paper.

At half past twelve we all spill out into the hallway. It feels like coming up for air. I avoid the post-exam dissections and head straight for the canteen where I've arranged to meet the others.

Over lunch, we catch up on the gossip from half-term. Aysha and Francine hang on every word as Lisa and I deliver a blow-by-blow account of everything that happened on Wednesday night.

'So did you both cop off then?' Aysha asks, desperate for the juicy details.

'Maybe,' Lisa teases her. 'Well, yeah, Steve and I got together.'

'I just like to take things slowly,' I say defensively, but then I grin when I think of Ian's awkward peck on the cheek. It's good to be one of the gang again. I feel an inch taller, as if there's a string pulling me upright, making me walk without touching the floor.

Ian catches up with me down by the lockers. I sidle away from the others, not wanting to be overheard. We lean against a draughty window that looks out on to the rain-flooded quad.

'So how was it?' he asks.

'You know. You always think you could have done better.'

'Yeah, I guess. I've got Spanish this afternoon.'

'Good luck.'

'Thanks, or *gracias*. I'll need it. I had my practical this morning. It was awful; all I could think of was French. My pronunciation was so dodgy.'

'Don't you get confused learning so many languages?'

'*Oui*. I mean *si*. There you go! I'm totally confused. I might as well just give up now.'

I laugh. He smiles at me with that wide mouth of his and I notice that his teeth are white and perfectly straight. He could be a toothpaste model with teeth like that. I start wondering whether there *is* such a thing as a toothpaste model.

'So are you done for the day?' he asks.

'Yeah.' I bump back down to earth. 'Kind of feels like skiving going home at lunch-time, but we've got geography tomorrow, and I really need to do some more revision before then.'

'And maths in the afternoon. Don't forget that.'

'Lucky us. No time off tomorrow then.'

'No. Well,' he sees Aysha, Francine and Lisa lurking in the background, 'I suppose I'll see you tomorrow. Maybe we can arrange to do something, you know, see a film or whatever.'

'That'd be nice,' I nod.

He smiles and runs off leaving Francine, Aysha and Lisa to swarm over me demanding to know every last thing he said. As if they haven't just earwigged every word!

When I get home, Mum is in the kitchen chopping vegetables. I make us both a cup of tea, while she witters on about the weather.

'I had my first exam today,' I remind her.

'Oh, yes, I meant to ask. It just slipped my mind. Do you think that's enough carrots?'

'Yeah, plenty. It went okay I think.'

'Well, that's good, love. I knew you'd be okay.' Mum has an empty way of talking; her words are colourless. She is too busy concentrating on dinner to pay any attention to me. I hate Colin for taking her away from me like this.

'Are you all right, Mum?'

'Yes. Of course I'm all right, love.' She laughs for good measure. 'I'm more than all right, in fact. My goodness, I wonder how long this rain is going to last?' she adds, eager to change the subject. 'Much more of this and we'll be washed away.'

I give up trying to make meaningful conversation and head upstairs with my tea and a cheese sandwich to reread my geography notes one last time. It's hard to concentrate and for once it's got nothing to do with this horrible house. I love the way Ian suddenly fills me up, runs through my mind, throwing out everything else, all the other crap. I want him to take me over completely so that there can be nothing else.

And yet, at the same time, that tiny voice at the back of my mind warns me off, tells me to be careful. You don't want to give too much of yourself away. People aren't always what they seem to be, what you'd like them to be, what you need them to be. I, of all people, should know that.

In the evening, when I feel like I can't read one more page, I take advantage of a break in the weather to go running. The streetlights glisten in the pools of water scattered along the pavements, the wetness squelching under my trainers. The park is so waterlogged I have to stick to the roads, running faster and further until I don't even bother to look where I'm going.

Eventually I pause to get my bearings, working out which way I need to run to get back home. Above me low charcoal clouds skate across the sky, blocking the stars from sight, making the world seem much smaller suddenly. They seem so close, it almost feels like they are pushing down on top of me. In the past, sailors used to navigate by looking up at the stars. They'd be screwed on a night like this, I think, as I pick up speed again and head for home.

Fourteen

The weather remains cold, accompanied by days on end of heavy, unyielding rain. Suddenly there are just six weeks till Christmas and all you can hear from the shops in town are the tinny strains of 'Merry Christmas Everybody' or 'Santa Claus is Coming To Town' or some other mind-numbing horror.

I don't get excited about the holidays. Maybe I used to when I was a kid, or in the early years when Colin was first on the scene and still on his best behaviour, but not any more. Now the thought of spending a week with us all together, pretending to be happy, leaves me cold and on edge. Christmas is worse than other holidays because you get the feeling that everyone else is having fun. You're supposed to 'enjoy yourself' whether you feel like it or not.

Ian and I are walking round town together in our lunch break. We have an extra half hour before our last exam. It's English, not the kind of thing you can revise for.

'Look at all this stuff.' I wave my hands at the racks and racks of Christmas tat: singing Santas, musical bobbing santas, revolving trees, fibre-optic trees that change colour every ten seconds.

'Not your kind of thing, then?'

'Are you kidding? Shops just want you to spend as much money as possible. That's why they bring out so much junk every year. I mean, it's not like anyone really *needs* a flashing-nose Rudolph or a Father Christmas that sings "Jingle Bells" in four different languages, is it?'

'Well, not *need*, no,' Ian admits. 'But, hey, it's Christmas.'

'I hate Christmas.'

'For real?'

'Yeah, why not,' I shrug. 'It's all just so... false.'

'Yeah, I suppose. But I kind of like it the way it is. It's more fun.' He comes up behind me wearing a set of flashing antlers. 'You just don't have a sense of humour.'

'Bah humbug,' I reply.

I know he's only kidding, but it bothers me just the same.

This is the third lunch-time we've spent together. Not exactly hot dates, but with exams and everything it's been hard to find the time. We're planning a foursome with Steve and Lisa at the weekend but we haven't worked out where to go yet. It's so cold and wet that no one feels like doing much. The nightly news rakes up statistics about the last time we had rain like this and they keep showing pictures of swollen rivers and people putting sandbags up around their houses. A flood alert phone number is flashed up at the bottom of the screen for worried people to call.

Not that Ian and I are worried. All we can focus on is the end of the exams. In fact I'd go so far as to say that for most of this week I've been on cloud nine. But then, of course, something will happen, someone says something or a thought just comes into my head out of nowhere and my whole mood comes crashing down again. It's like being on a roller coaster, one moment up, next moment down. What Lisa said about me being moody still bugs me. Now I think, maybe she's right.

We sit in the exam room as the teachers place papers on all the desks. Francine swivels round in her chair, grins at Lisa, looks over at Steve then back to Lisa again. Aysha smiles across too. It's weird. I've gone from being on the edge of things to right back in the middle, just like before, but it doesn't feel the same somehow.

'You want to do something this evening, just the two of us?' Ian leans over to me. 'We could go into town and look at the lights. Doesn't have to be a late one.'

Miss Parkinson raps on the desk with a bundle of spare pens and all eyes turn towards her.

'I'll take that as a yes then?' Ian hisses when I don't reply.

'Ian Barker, if you wouldn't mind letting us get on,' Miss Parkinson sighs tiredly.

'Bri!' he whispers. 'What d'you say?'

I look anxiously from Miss P to him. 'Yes, okay. God!'

And he grins that big wide grin of his that makes me melt inside.

'Mum, you know I wouldn't ask if it wasn't important.'

My mother bustles round the kitchen to avoid looking me directly in the eye.

'And *you* know that Colin likes us all to sit down together in the evening.'

'What about David? Half the time he doesn't even come home and no one says anything to him.'

'You're not your brother.'

'How come it's always different for David?'

'Because it is, Briony. Because he's older. Because he's a boy.'

'Oh, please!' I shake my head in disbelief.

'And anyway, just because Colin doesn't say anything, doesn't mean he's happy with it.'

But for once I am not prepared to bend just to keep the peace.

'It'd only be for a couple of hours.'

'You need to eat properly, especially in this weather. Besides, it's still raining.'

'So, I'll wear a hat! And we'll get some chips.'

'Chips is not a proper meal. Anyway, we don't even know this Ian boy.'

I wonder if she really wants me to invite him over. I can't imagine it. Visitors have never been made very welcome in our house. Colin doesn't like surprises, people he doesn't know.

I can feel her weakening, the way my mother always does when someone stands up to her. It gives me a funny, uncomfortable feeling in the pit of my stomach.

'But what am I going to say to Colin?' she pleads. 'It'll just be the two of us if David's late again.'

'So?' He's *your* husband, I feel like saying.

She looks at me and I throw it back at her the way my brother does with me.

'Anyway, Colin told me himself I should go out more.'

'He did?'

'Yeah, he said all work and no play makes Jill a dull girl.'

Mum looks at me with those silently screaming eyes of hers but I push myself off the counter and get ready. I know she won't stop me.

'Hey.'

Ian jumps off the wall outside the station where we've arranged to meet.

'Hey, yourself.'

The air is so cold it takes your breath away but at least the rain has finally stopped.

'I was beginning to think you weren't going to show.'

'Am I late?'

He gives me a peck on the cheek. 'Maybe just a bit. But you're here now.'

'My mum wasn't exactly keen on me coming out tonight.'

'No? Your folks sound really strict.'

'Yeah, they are, kind of.'

He slips his hand into mine. 'So shall we go and look at the Christmas tree in the centre or will that be too fake and commercial for you?'

'Probably, but I know it's the kind of thing you like,' I tease and we set off to marvel at how the council have transformed our town with the aid of some tacky lights and cheap, plastic Santas.

On the way we stop for chips at Pete's Plaice. The hot vinegar smell wafts out into the freezing air, a million miles from the strained mealtime I'd be suffering back home. It maybe doesn't sound like much but it's another of those moments that I'd love to stuff into my bottle of memories.

We walk through St George's Park, and follow the path of the swollen river, which crosses the park and flows on to the lower end of town.

'So come on, tell me your life story,' Ian says through hot chips. 'I've seen you in school every day for the last five years and I still don't know much about you.'

'Yeah, but that's just how it is at school, isn't it?'

He looks at me. 'S'pose so. Funny isn't it, how you can know someone and not know them at the same time?'

'Well, I don't know anything about you either.'

'Ah, but you see I *knew* you were going to do that,' he says triumphantly. 'You always do that when I ask you something. It's like you don't want anyone to know anything about you.'

'Oh, very deep,' I scoff. 'When did you start taking psychology lessons?'

'I thought I was doing quite well.'

'I don't know what you want to know anyway. I don't think there's much to tell.'

'Favourite food, favourite colour – '

'We did all that the last time. Anyway, that kind of stuff isn't important.'

'No? Well, what is?'

'I don't know. But you don't get to know someone by knowing what their favourite colour is.'

'So how do I get to know you? You intrigue me.'

'*Intrigue* you? Are you sure?' I shoot him my most sceptical look.

'You always put yourself down,' he replies solemnly. 'Have you noticed that?'

I shrug, not wanting to take anything too seriously tonight.

'Maybe you think that if you get in first, it'll stop everyone else from doing it.'

'Oh, please, spare me the analysis.'

'Well, that's usually why people put themselves down.'

'And how do you know so much about it, Professor Barker?'

'My mum's a social worker. I've read some of her books.'

I shake my head. 'Yeah, well, maybe you should wait until you understand all the long words.'

Ian glances sideways at me, grinning. 'I'm still intrigued.'

'You need help.'

'Yeah, probably,' he laughs.

The night is cold and still and the rain has left the ground boggy and slippery. It's not surprising the park is deserted except for the two of us.

'I've never seen the river so full,' says Ian as we pick our way carefully through the puddles. 'You think it's going to flood?'

'Won't be the first if it does. I saw one place on the news tonight, a village with sandbags on the doorsteps and the army evacuating people with inflatable dinghies. It was mad.' I angle my watch face up to the light to see how long I've been out.

'Don't tell me you've got to go already.' Ian bins our chip wrappers then slings his arm around me. 'Stick with me. I'll warm you up.'

'I told you what my parents are like. I can't be late.'

'You're *not* late! Your parents can't be that strict. It's only just gone half past seven.'

'Late enough.' I look down, avoiding his eyes. 'Anyway, it's just my stepfather really. He can be a bit funny sometimes. And, for your information, it's already quarter to eight.'

'You don't get on with him?'

'Who?'

'Your stepfather.'

'Not much.'

'So? Talk to me about it.'

'There you go again. What did I just say?'

'That I'm the best looking guy in our school?'

'Did I really say that? Funny, I don't remember saying anything like that.'

And that's when we both hear it: a whimpering, frightened, crying sort of sound. And it's coming from the river's edge.

Fifteen

The water is almost all the way up to the top of the riverbank. On the other side, a dog is racing up and down the grass, barking.

'Oh, shit, it's just a dog,' Ian gasps. 'I thought for a moment...'

'Shhh, there's somebody out there.' I point towards a dark shape struggling in the shadows by the far bank.

'What the hell are they doing?'

'I think it's a kid. They must have fallen in.'

As our eyes adjust to the darkness by the water's edge, we can definitely see a figure clinging to an overhanging bush. The water is flowing fast and high, swollen by days of rain. The little dog edges towards the child, begins to slip on the muddy ground and scrambles back up to safety, yapping all the time.

'You've got a mobile phone, haven't you? We need to call somebody,' I say, my breath coming in ragged little gasps.

Ian fumbles frantically in his jeans pocket.

'It's okay! We're going to get help!' I shout across the river.

The child, a girl, is crying now, gripping onto the branches of the bush for all she's worth in order to stop herself from being pulled into the muddy torrent. I edge as close to the river as I can but there's no way of reaching her.

'You think one of us could get across?' I wonder.

'Even if you could stand up in there, the current would probably sweep you downstream in no time.' Ian punches the buttons on his phone. 'Briony – '

'Just call the police, will you?' I urge him.

I've got to find some way of getting across to that girl. The river's not particularly wide and under normal circumstances I could probably walk to the other side, but tonight everything's different. As I near the water I can feel its icy wetness licking through my trainers. The kid must be freezing out there.

At the far end of the park I know there's a bridge. It seems like our only hope. I take off at a sprint, my feet slipping and sliding as I slither across the water-sodden ground.

'Briony! Where are you going?' Ian breaks off from his phone call, shouting after me.

There's no time to stop and explain. He'll figure it out.

I almost fall on my face several times and am splattered with cold, wet mud by the time I hurl myself across the bridge. I fix my eyes on the dog ahead of me, sprinting back level to where Ian is standing.

'The police and an ambulance are coming!' Ian shouts over the gushing of the river. 'Don't do anything stupid, Bri.'

The little girl is up to her chest in water, desperately gripping on to a handful of bent branches that trail limply into the river. I bend down to reach her, the dog snapping excitedly at my heels. Suddenly, without warning, the muddy bank gives way.

I gasp as the cold water slices through my body. Frantically I make a grab for the bank, feeling the water tugging violently at my legs, wanting to take me away. I am surprised by how strong the current is.

The child whimpers, just an arm's length away from me. She hasn't got the strength to pull herself back up to safety; it's all she can do to hang on.

'Don't let go!' I shout to her. 'I'm going to get you out!'

I wade towards her, stumbling deeper into the water as I lose my footing on the uneven riverbed. I know that I cannot afford to fall. If I do, the water will have me. My numb hands reach frantically for clumps of grass or roots – anything I can use to anchor myself.

Finally, I reach the girl and stand directly in front of her with one arm on either side, my fingers digging into the soil of the bank behind her. Her feet kick against me. She's gasping, straining to keep her head out of the water but she can't hold on much longer. My mind races. I don't know if I am strong enough to support us both, but I can see that she is just about ready to give up.

'You think you can put your hands around my neck?' Her eyes are screwed shut and she doesn't appear to hear me. 'Take one hand and grab on to me!' My voice doesn't sound like mine. I have no strength to get the words out.

Finally, one hand loosens slightly on the branches and flails towards me eventually hooking on to my jacket. I feel the extra weight of her.

'Try to put your legs round my waist.'

'I can't,' she cries, teeth chattering.

I don't know what else to do. I am rooted to the spot, only just managing to hang on to the bank myself. If I move, the two of us might go under.

And then I hear Ian's voice again, much closer this time. I look up and see that he is lying on the ground beside the overhanging bush, stretching his arms out towards us.

'Take the girl!' My voice is shrill above the noise of the river.

Ian swears as he grabs a hold, first of me, then the little girl and tries to haul her towards him. She fights, scared to let go, and in the confusion kicks me as her frozen body twists towards the muddy bank. I lose my hold and fall backwards into the rushing water. I feel it in my ears, my eyes, inside my skull and I lunge forward, trying desperately to get back to the bank. But the river is quicker than I am.

Intense cold seems to blot out everything else. I feel my body spinning round and around and I bump against something, a tangle of tree roots. I grope blindly for them, feel my fingers curl round something wet and cold, and manage to get my feet back onto the river floor, my head straining upwards, gasping and spitting for breath.

'Briony!' I hear Ian's frightened voice calling out through the darkness.

The air around me is raw against my wet skin and hair. My head aches with the cold. The rest of me is numb, stiff. It no longer feels like my body. I scrabble for a foothold as my feet slide away from me once more but my fingers are locked on to the roots of the tree beside me and I manage to hold firm. Time stands still, every minute an hour. I can barely breathe and feel myself beginning to slip into unconsciousness.

'Briony!'

'Okay, we're here, just hold on.'

A voice I don't recognise materialises out of the blackness and suddenly someone is beside me, struggling to pull me out of the water. My fingers are so numb that I can't let go of the root and my hands have to be prised free. Someone helps me onto the bank and I collapse, exhausted.

Sixteen

I am sitting in the casualty ward of the local hospital, swathed in blankets and drinking hot, sugary tea. My mind is all fuzzy and it seems to take forever to warm up again. The nurses tell me that both the kid, a nine-year-old girl called Amy and the dog, a terrier puppy called Caesar, are doing well. But I'm too exhausted to register any kind of emotion.

Mum and Colin appear shortly afterwards with a bundle of clean clothes. I stiffen, watching for clues as to how they are going to react.

'Briony, love, are you all right?' Mum takes my hand in hers and rubs it frantically. 'What did you think you were doing?' Her eyes are wide and round.

'I guess I didn't think.'

'It was either very brave or very stupid,' Colin remarks coldly.

'Well, let's just be thankful she's okay,' breathes Mum.

'Makes no sense putting yourself in danger to rescue someone else.'

'Yeah, well, someone had to do something,' I mutter.

A nurse comes in and stands at the end of the bed, smiling warmly at the three of us.

'You must be so proud of your daughter. She's very brave.'

'Of course we are, very proud, aren't we, love?' Mum glances at Colin. 'We were just saying as much. It sets my heart going just thinking about what might have happened.'

Colin rests his hand protectively on Mum's shoulder. 'I still can't imagine what made her do it, what she was thinking of.'

'Well, I guess sometimes you don't think when you're in that kind of situation. Isn't that right?' the nurse says turning to me.

'Suppose.' I drop my eyes.

'Let's all just thank the Lord that she's okay,' my dear stepfather smiles and this somehow signals an end to the conversation.

'Amen to that.' The nurse nods, reaching for her thermometer.

I look at Col as if he's a stranger. It's been so long since I've seen him outside the house. I don't recognise this Colin, the Colin that the rest of the world sees. Just as I put on my mask when I enter the school gates, so Colin must play a different role when he is away from us. The nice man. The reasonable man. The nurse waves my temperature away, smiles, and reaches for my empty plastic beaker.

'Here, let me take that for you. I expect you'll feel better when you get some warm clothes on.'

I swing my legs down off the bed, pull the blankets tighter around me.

'Has the girl's father spoken to you? I know he was keen to thank you.'

I shake my head and my brain rattles around inside my skull.

'He's about somewhere. You want me to see if I can

find him? I know it would mean a lot to him.'

I look to Colin, as I always do, silently asking permission, seeing if it's okay.

'We'll wait out front for you,' he nods and guides Mum away.

I stay where I am, sitting on the edge of the bed, tired and thinking how strange everything feels. Slowly I put on my clothes.

'Hey, Bri!' Ian pokes his head round the curtain. 'Oh, shame, you're decent.'

'I'm just about to go home.'

'Yeah, me too. My parents are here. So are you okay?'

'I wish everyone would stop asking me that.'

'What d'you want them to ask you, your favourite colour?'

I throw him a look.

'Hey, I saw your parents out in the corridor.' Ian lowers his voice. 'They came over and said hello to me, you know, when I was talking to that nurse.' He adds, almost apologetically, 'They seemed nice.'

'Well, what were you expecting?'

'I dunno, maybe a Nazi uniform and Hitler moustache.'

'Don't say things like that!' I hiss back. 'And keep your voice down.'

'It was just a joke, Bri.'

'Yeah, well, whatever.'

It's funny that other people don't see what I see when they look at my stepfather, but then they don't know what I know. It makes me feel like a fraud, as if I've made everything up.

'Are you okay for another visitor?' The nurse pops her head back round the curtain.

A man I don't know comes in. I guess it's the little girl's

father. He's younger than Colin, with brown hair and kind eyes behind narrow, rectangular glasses.

'Am I interrupting? I just wanted to say thank you for what you did.'

'It's nothing really.' I smile, embarrassed.

'I don't know about that. If it hadn't been for the two of you, Amy might never have made it.'

I look away, uncomfortable with his kind eyes and grateful smile.

'She knows she's not allowed out of the house on her own after dark, but the puppy got out and well, I suppose you can guess the rest.' He laughs, shaking his head and pulling his hands through his hair. 'Anyway, that's kids for you. Don't know whether to hug her or strangle her.'

He smiles at me and I manage to grimace back at him, then look down at the shiny, grey floor tiles.

'Well, I don't really know what to say. Thank you somehow doesn't seem adequate. I feel like I should do something for you, try to show you my appreciation, even if it's just inviting you both over for dinner one night. I'm sure Amy would like to say thank you too.'

'I don't know,' I stumble, automatically searching for a get-out clause. 'I mean, you really don't have to.'

'But I want to,' he says. 'Here, I have a card.' He pulls out his wallet and hands Ian and me two business cards. I notice that his hands are shaking. 'Perhaps you'll give me a call when you feel up to it. I really want to repay you for what you've done. It's not every day that someone saves my daughter's life.'

I stare at the little white card in my hands. My nails are still caked in mud.

'Yeah, thanks Mr Graham,' says Ian. 'We'll do that.'

And with that Mr Mike Graham, (M.Sc. CEng.) makes

his excuses and backs awkwardly out of the cubicle.

'D'you hear that Bri?' Ian leans over to me. 'Repay us? I am sensing the unmistakable odour of money here.' He kisses me. 'Anyway, I've got to go. My parents are out in the carpark. I'll call you, yeah?'

'Yeah.' I wonder when I gave him my phone number. 'Yeah, see you.'

And I watch him go, wondering why I still feel nothing at all.

Seventeen

'You've got a visitor.' Mum pokes her mousy head round my bedroom door. It's Saturday morning and I'm lazing around in bed. Mum stands aside and Lisa waltzes casually into my room.

'Oh, Bri, I came as soon as I heard. Are you all right? What happened?'

She flops down on my bed and makes herself comfortable. I clear away a pile of magazines and books.

'Heard from who?'

'Steve. Ian phoned him this morning and he phoned me. I came straight over. You're not busy, are you?'

'No, I was just reading.'

I feel invaded. She shouldn't be here. This belongs to my private world that she knows nothing about; the two sides of me I keep completely separate.

'So, come on, Bri. Tell me everything.'

Reluctantly I tell her about last night and she listens with wide eyes and this weird, excitable look on her face. When I have finished she shakes her head. Lots of people have been shaking their heads at me lately.

'God, you are *so* brave.'

'But that's just it! I'm not!'

'You are too,' she insists. 'God!'

I feel unworthy of all this praise.

'I wouldn't be surprised if the local paper doesn't do a story on you. You might even be on TV.'

'Get real.'

'This is real, Bri. You're a hero. Heroine. Whatever.'

'I probably wouldn't have gone into the river if I hadn't actually fallen in. It's all a big mistake.'

'Hark at Miss Modesty over here,' Lisa tuts. 'I'm telling you, this is just *so* cool. I've never known anyone nearly famous before.'

'Oh, is that what I am now?'

'Sure. God, Bri, I wish I'd been there. It's one hell of a story.'

'If you say so.'

There's a bleeping coming from her jacket pocket. I know immediately what that means. Lisa has joined the ranks of Francine and Aysha and everyone else I know and got herself a mobile phone. She pulls out this tiny yellow number, looks at the screen and giggles.

'Ah, sweet. It's Steve.'

She passes the phone over to me so I can read his message.

RUF2T OR TXT?

'Am I missing something here?' I hand it back.

She speed dials his number.

'You're gonna have to get yourself a phone, Bri, you really are. Yeah, hi, it's me... no, I'm at Briony's... yeah, she was just telling me about it... yeah... yeah... okay, hold on.' She passes the phone back to me. 'He wants to speak to you himself.'

'Hi, Steve,' I drawl in my best bored tone. 'No it's okay... yeah? No, I'm not an invalid, you know... no, well it was kind of scary now that I look back on it, but it wasn't at the time if you know what I mean...'

Lisa gets up and wanders round my room, looking at stuff. I watch her suspiciously as I talk.

'He did? Oh, right...no, I think I'm going to have a quiet one, you know with everything that's happened ...okay then.' I hold the phone out to Lisa.'He wants to speak to you again.'

'Are you not coming out tonight, Bri?' she asks.'Hello, yeah...yeah...well, we can always do something, can't we? Okay, babe. See you later.'

'*Babe*?' I gag. 'When did you two get to the twee-names stage?' I mimic her on the phone and she throws a box of tissues at me.

'You're just jealous that you and Ian aren't like me and Steve.'

'What, sick-making?'

'Say what you like, I don't care. I'm happy.'

She wafts around my room, fingering ornaments on the window sill, the junk on my dressing table.

'You know, I love looking round people's rooms, especially dressing tables. I think you can tell a lot about a person just from the stuff they have lying around.'

I shift awkwardly on my bed.'Oh yeah? And what does mine tell you about me?'

Lisa shrugs, dismissively.'I dunno. It's too neat for my liking.'

'Just 'cos you live in a sty.'

'Thanks a lot, *mate*.' She looks out of the window, inside the wardrobe, examines every corner of my room. 'God, I can't remember the last time I was in your house, Bri. I forgot how huge it is.You're really lucky, you know? I mean you've seen the size of my bedroom. I've had shoes come in bigger boxes than my room.' She comes across my CD player and a small stack of CDs sitting on the floor. 'Mind if I put something on?' I nod and she sticks a CD in the machine, points the remote control at it and fiddles with the volume. 'This is the greatest. I love this first track. It's definitely my favourite.'

Music blares out. I had no idea that the volume could go so high. Usually I keep it down to a one or a two. She has it up on four. I fumble the control off her and deaden the sound.

'We're not the only ones in the house, you know.'

'So? I don't suppose you can hear anything downstairs. Not like my house. My dad farts in the night and wakes up next door's cat!'

'Colin doesn't like me playing music too loud,' I mutter.

'Yeah? And what's he gonna do?'

Suddenly I don't want Lisa to be here. I don't want to have to explain myself, make excuses for the way things are. I flip through a magazine, willing her to go.

'So, d'you think you will get yourself a phone?' Lisa pulls out her mobile again, and starts tapping in a text message to lover-boy. 'It'd be so cool if you did. We could all text each other: you and me and Steve and Ian and Francine and Aysha. It'd be excellent.'

As always I'm the outsider, the one who's different from everyone else, this time because I don't have a mobile phone.

'Who knows?' I shrug vaguely.

'Yeah, I suppose Christmas is coming up. Maybe your mum'll buy you one, huh?'

'Maybe.'

We sit like this for a bit longer, her and Steve swapping pukey messages until I finally freeze her out and she decides to go. I see her down to the front door, closing it with a heavy sigh. Mum is there at the kitchen door with a tea towel in her hands and a forced smile on her face.

'Well, that was a surprise, wasn't it? Did you invite her over, love? You should have told us if you were going to have friends over.'

'She just came, Mum. It's no big deal.'

But of course everything is a big deal in our house.

Eighteen

It never rains but it pours. I've just got rid of Lisa and taken a short walk to clear my head when I see Ian ambling up the road towards my house. I sprint to catch up with him.

'Jesus, you're a bit keen aren't you? I thought after yesterday you wouldn't be up to running.'

'What are you doing here?' I wheeze.

'I've been trying to call you all morning but I couldn't get through. Is there something wrong with your phone?'

For a moment or two I just stare at him. 'Yeah, actually there is.'

Like the toast rack and the blue china flower vase before it, the phone has never been replaced.

'So how are you today? Have you thought any more about contacting that man, Amy's dad?'

'It was only yesterday. God, give me a chance.' I bite down a sudden flash of irritation. 'How did you get my phone number anyway?'

'I don't know, you must have given it to me, or Lisa did.' He looks at me expectantly. 'Well, are you going to invite me in?'

'What?'

'Inside.' He jerks his head towards the house. 'It's bloody freezing out here.'

I want to get rid of him but my brain flounders uselessly in its search for a believable excuse. I feel the two worlds I inhabit come crashing together, crowding in on me.

'Come on, your parents like me, remember?'

I smile weakly and lead him round the back to the kitchen. Mum comes scurrying through when she hears the back door.

'Briony, love, I thought I heard someone.' Her eyes flick anxiously between Ian and me.

'Hello, Mrs Newman,' Ian beams innocently.

She falters. 'Er... Miriam, please,' she says awkwardly and I cringe.

'She's Mrs *Bliss*,' I mutter to the floor. 'So d'you want a drink?'

Ian is completely oblivious to the tension stretched like an invisible elastic band around our house.

'Briony, perhaps your friend would like some of the cranberry juice I got yesterday? It's in the fridge.'

'Yeah, okay.' I wish Mum would just go and leave us alone. She makes me feel uncomfortable because I know *she's* uncomfortable.

Colin slopes in from the sitting room and looks at the three of us. He's obviously ill at ease to find yet another person he doesn't know in his lair.

'It's Briony's friend,' Mum tells him quickly, at pains to make everything look normal for Ian. 'You remember? We saw him at the hospital yesterday?'

'I'm not a complete idiot, Miriam. I haven't quite got to that age when I can't remember things from one day to the next.'

Ian laughs. He thinks Colin's being funny. Maybe he is.

'Would you like tea, love? I can put the kettle on,' Mum pants. 'Ian, I expect you'll have some tea, will you?'

'Yeah, tea or juice, whatever.' He shrugs.

'I'll make tea. Why don't you go and sit down, Colin, love? I'll bring it through when it's ready.'

'Oh, I see. Like that is it? I know when I'm not wanted.'

Ian laughs again as my stepfather goes sulking back to his corner.

Mum bustles past me, fills the kettle from the tap, plugs it in. Her eyes catch mine just once and I know she's upset that I've brought two strangers in without asking permission.

'Ian was just outside when I came back,' I try to explain.

She fakes a happy face. 'Well, it's always nice to meet your friends from school,' she lies chirpily, turning to Ian. 'Briony's such a loner.'

I can feel my face redden. I'm angry with her for embarrassing me like that, for making out that people can drop in whenever they like, for not supporting me after all the support I've given her.

'D'you blame me?' I mutter, sourly.

'Anyway, your father's had a hard week at work, love, so I'd appreciate it if you could both keep the noise down a bit.'

'Sure.' I stare back at her until she is forced to look away.

Ian and I take two mugs of tea and half a packet of chocolate digestives up to my room but leave the door open in case anyone gets any bright ideas. Ian sips at his mug.

'So how come your mum calls your stepfather your father? He's not, is he?'

'No.' My skin prickles. 'I guess that's just the illusion she wants to create. I don't know.' I catch the way he's looking at me. 'And don't start with all your psychological crap again.'

'Did you get out of bed the wrong side this morning or something?' Ian retorts defensively. He looks around my room. 'You've got a nice place here.'

I look away. I don't want him poking around my bedroom the way Lisa did this morning. I feel on edge, but try my best to conceal it.

'So, are you coming out tonight?' he asks.

'I've already told Lisa and Steve that I'm staying home.'

'Yeah? You seen them?'

'Lisa called round this morning. Steve phoned up while she was here.' I put my face into the steam from my mug, giving my pores a quick facial. 'How come you knew where I lived anyway?'

Ian acts like he hasn't given it much thought. 'I asked Lisa. She told me.'

I nod. 'Seems like everyone spends a lot of time talking about me.'

'I asked her for your address,' he says coolly, 'not your life story. What's wrong with you today? I only stopped by because I was worried about you.'

'There's nothing wrong with me. God!'

I stomp anxiously around my room wishing everyone would just leave me alone. Ian watches me with a frown on his face. He doesn't understand. I feel like a cornered animal with him sitting there like that.

'I'm sorry. I didn't realise calling round would be such a big hassle.'

I wheel round. 'It's not. Why d'you say that? I don't care if you come round here or not.'

I didn't mean that to come out quite the way it did. I gnaw on my lip, unable to take it back. Ian looks hurt.

'Yeah, right, thanks a lot. You obviously don't want me here.'

I take a deep breath. 'I saw you only yesterday. Just because we're going out doesn't mean we have to live in each other's pockets.'

Ian stares at me with wounded eyes. 'I didn't think we were.' He sets his mug down on my dressing table. 'But I'll get going then. See you around, Bri.'

He turns and makes for the stairs. My stomach twists into knots. I want to ask him to stay but I can't find the words. He leaves, slamming the door behind him.

'So, are we going to have any more visitors dropping in on us today?' I jump. Colin has a horrible way of sneaking up on people.

'No. I shouldn't think so,' I say as I fill the kettle to make myself another cup of tea.

'I hope not because I'm getting sick of being made to feel like a stranger in my own home,' he snaps.

I keep my back to him. Don't want to apologise. Don't want to make him a cup of tea. Don't want to have anything to do with him. He might be able to fool Mum, but he can't fool me.

Drawn to the kitchen by the sound of our voices, Mum flutters in the doorway.

'What time is dinner? I'm bloody starving,' Colin growls at her.

'Well it'll take me an hour or so.' Mum jumps. 'Perhaps I can make you a sandwich. Cheese and ham, okay?'

I hate that tone of hers, determinedly upbeat no matter what. But Colin does not want to be appeased with a sandwich. He wants to make an issue of this. He chews over her offer.

'I'll start on the dinner.' Mum falls into the kitchen, ever ready to fulfil her wifely duties.

'I'll have a sandwich,' he grunts. 'Egg mayonnaise.'

'Right.' Mum switches back into sandwich-mode. 'Egg mayonnaise it is.'

'And Briony can make it.'

Both she and I falter. So that's his game.

'It's no trouble...' Mum begins.

'I said I want *her* to make it.'

Mum looks at me with pleading eyes, begging me to keep the peace. I shrug my shoulders. Already I'm reaching for the fridge. Like mother, like daughter.

The smell of hard-boiled eggs makes me want to retch. I shell them into the bin and run cold water over them. My fingers burn.

'Remember the black pepper, love,' Mum whispers helpfully over my shoulder. 'Salt and pepper, and just a little bit of marge. Use Flora.'

'I do know how to make a sandwich, you know.'

'I know. But Colin can be so particular about things.'

'Miriam!' Col summons my mother as if he's been listening to us from the sitting room.

Then I do something I know I shouldn't, but I do it just the same. I spit into the egg mayonnaise mixture. I beat it hastily with a fork, then spread it out over his neatly Flora-ed squares of bread, a faint feeling of satisfaction rising warmly inside me.

I take the sandwich through to the sitting room where Mum and Colin are drinking tea. I go to put it on the floor beside his chair but he motions that he wants it now.

As much as I don't like being in the same room as my stepfather, I very much want to see him take that first bite, so I hang around, perching myself on the arm of the other chair, pretending to read the TV pages. He takes the sandwich unwittingly in his giant shovel hands and chomps down. A moment later he leaps out of his chair, spraying mouthfuls of egg mayonnaise over the carpet. I watch, horrified. Surely he can't taste my spit in there?

'What are you trying to do? Poison me?' He gags, his face stormy, tongue lolling out like a dog's.

I get uneasily to my feet.

'What is it, Colin?' Mum asks, nervously.

'Shell!' he explodes. 'Bloody shell. The bitch was trying to choke me!'

When I realise that this has nothing to do with me gobbing into his sarnie I feel a moment of relief. It must show. Colin's hand comes down hard across the side of my mouth.

'Think it's funny do you?' he hollers.

'Colin, no!' Mum leaps to her feet.

All three of us pause for a second, standing absolutely still. My mouth feels smeared across my face. I daren't breathe, make any kind of movement in case it entices him to slap me again.

'She was bloody laughing,' Colin barks.

'I wasn't.'

Mum is suddenly the adjudicator in the dispute and she falters as she realises the delicate predicament she is in. I look at her, my hand against my cheek where I can still feel his thick fingers, look at her for some kind of support, united against the enemy, but she drops her eyes from mine, just like I knew she was going to do, and goes instead to pick up the remnants of egg mayonnaise from the floor.

As much as I hate to give that bastard any kind of satisfaction at all, I can feel hot pools forming behind my eyes, tears dropping onto my stinging cheek. I don't know if I'm more angry at him for hitting me or my mother for not saying anything. I mutter something under my breath, then bolt for the front door.

I make sure it rattles long and hard behind me.

Nineteen

It's cold outside. Too cold to be out with no coat and nowhere to go. So I head for the only place I can think of. Lisa's. Her mother answers the door. I hope she can't tell I've been crying.

'Well, well, if it's not our very own local hero! Come on in, Briony. My goodness, you look half frozen to death.'

'Thanks, Mrs Stanley. Is Lisa in?'

'Lisa!' she hollers up the stairs, then turns back to me. 'Did you come out without a coat?' She shakes her head as Lisa appears. 'Teenagers, I'll never understand them. My God, doesn't that make me sound old?'

'Hey, what are you doing here?' Lisa swings down off the stairs, ushering me back up to her bedroom. 'Are you all right, Bri? You look kinda weird.'

As she shuts the door behind us and the warmth of her house begins to penetrate, I know I'm going to start crying again, which is ridiculous because the Briony Newman that Lisa Stanley knows just doesn't behave like that. I bury my head in my hands.

'Briony, what's happened? Tell me. God, you're scaring me!'

I open my mouth to speak but for some reason I can't stop blubbing. Eventually, Lisa thrusts a pack of tissues into my hand and I pull myself together.

'Everything's just going wrong,' I croak.

She looks at me, her face full of concern, waiting for me to explain.

'Ian came round. We had a fight. I think we've split up.'

'Oh, Bri!' Lisa sinks down beside me and hugs me. 'God, you really do like him, don't you? I had no idea it was that serious between you.'

I shrug. It wasn't, or isn't. But it's as good as anything else to cry about.

Lisa's mum cooks us burgers and oven chips and then Lisa calls Steve on her mobile and asks him if he's seen Ian. Surprise, surprise, he's there, at Steve's place.

'You want to speak to him?' she mouths but I shake my head.

She takes the phone out of the room, no doubt to explain the full story to lover-boy and then comes back a minute or so later looking very pleased with herself.

'Okay, that's settled then. We're meeting Steve at seven-thirty, down at the Corn Exchange.'

'Like I don't know Ian's going to be there,' I snuffle. 'I know when I'm being set up, Lise.'

'Well, of course he's going to be there!' She rolls her eyes at me. 'D'oh! I mean, do you want to get back with him or not?'

I nod, even though I don't feel sure of anything anymore. I nod because that's what's expected of me and, after all, I'm only playing a role. Perhaps we all are.

'Hey. Didn't think I'd be seeing you again so soon.'

'Yeah, well.' I shrug uselessly.

We are at the Corn Exchange Arcade, a cool place to hang out if you've got money to burn on the games. Lisa drags Steve off towards the Bowlingo! while me and Ian head for the little café area. We grab a coffee and a hot chocolate and sit there awkwardly, not knowing what to say to each other.

'So?' Ian prompts.

'So, I guess I just wanted to say sorry for snapping at you this afternoon. I didn't mean for it to sound the way it did.' I take off the jacket Lisa has lent me and hang it over the back of the chair, anything to avoid looking at him.

'It sounded like you didn't want to go out with me any more,' he observes coldly.

'I know. I didn't mean it like that.'

'So how did you mean it?'

'I don't know.' I pick up my steaming chocolate but it's still too hot to drink. 'Things are just really complicated for me at the minute.'

'So, do you want us to carry on seeing each other or not?' he asks.

There's a pause.

'Yes.' I hear myself say, and it's true, I think.

I do want to keep seeing him just as I want to do all the other normal stuff that people my age do — go for long walks and share secrets and phone each other late at night and sit next to each other in the form room giggling and mucking around — but then my life is not like other people's.

'But what?' Ian asks. 'Don't tell me there's not a but coming because I can see it in your face.'

'But nothing,' I lie. 'It's just...'

'Yeah, here we go.'

'It's just my life is not great at the moment, okay?' I snap at him. 'You caught me at a bad time, that's all. My stepfather and I are going through a bit of a bad patch.'

Ian doesn't say anything. It's like he's weighing my words up, deciding whether I'm telling the truth or just trying to let him down gently.

'We had a row today and he hit me,' I blurt out.

'He hit you? Why?'

I look away, wonder what Ian would do if he knew the way things really are at home.

'What's going on?' Ian catches my arm and tries to look me in the eye.

'My stepfather hit me because I got eggshell in his sandwich.'

'Jesus! That's child abuse!'

'Don't be daft.' I burn my tongue on the hot chocolate. 'It was just a slap. And I spat in his sandwich anyway, so I guess I probably deserved it.'

'You *what*?'

'I spat in his sandwich.'

Ian leans back in his chair, staring at me. 'I don't know what to make of you Bri, I really don't.'

'Yeah, well, just don't get me to make you a sandwich.'

'No I won't, don't worry. I definitely won't.' He's still looking hard at me, searching out the truth, the way I do with Mum sometimes.

'Look it's nothing. Over. Done. Don't worry about it. I'm just telling you because today was a bad day. That's why everything got so messed up. I was just in a really foul mood, okay?'

'And you're all right now?'

'I'm fine. Honest.'

He nods slowly, taking it all on board. Suddenly I feel just like Mum, covering it all up, but what else can I do?

When we have finished our drinks we have a couple of goes at air hockey, then the four of us go bowling and finally end up blowing any remaining cash on the DDR machine, making complete prats of ourselves, jumping about one step behind the music and the animated figures on the screen. But it doesn't matter. Because as long as we are all here, then there *is* nothing else, just this arcade and the four of us having a laugh, and everything else is unimportant.

It's about ten-thirty when I get home, still wearing Lisa's jacket. The street is quiet and there's no movement apart from the odd cat darting in and out of the shadows. As I head up the drive I notice that the garage door is up and Colin's car is out. It hits me like a fist to the stomach. It's too late for him to be out normally. I wonder, with a sick kind of feeling, if something is wrong.

I turn my key in the front-door lock and step into the darkened hallway. My trainers crunch over the carpet. Flicking on the hall light, I find the floor covered in shards of smashed glass from a photo that usually stands on the little side table by the door. The picture itself is strewn in raggedy bits among the glass. It was a photo of me, Mum and David taken at the beach years ago. My stomach washes with acid.

'Mum?' I stumble through to the living room, the blood draining out of me.

My mother is sitting in an armchair with her back to me. She looks as though she's watching TV except the set isn't on. Her head is resting on one hand and she doesn't even seem to notice me as I approach. When I come round to face her I can see that she's been crying.

'What's he done, Mum?' I search frantically for the cuts and bruises.

She sniffles into a tissue; continues staring straight ahead.

'Did he hit you?' I kneel down beside her.

'I'm okay, Bri.'

'But the photo out in the hall?'

'We had an argument. You know what Colin's like. He stormed out and I guess it was just in his way.'

'But did he hurt you, Mum?'

'He didn't hit me if that's what you mean,' she answers, distantly.

There's something about her tonight that sends a shiver under my skin.

'What happened?'

'Does it matter?' Her red eyes flick just once over to me, then go back to staring fixedly in front of her. 'He shouldn't have hit you, Briony. What he did was wrong.'

'You told him that?' I gasp but she doesn't reply.

Eventually she glances back at me. 'That's not your jacket.'

'No, it's Lisa's. She lent it to me.'

'You left in such a hurry.'

'Do you blame me?'

She closes her eyes. 'I've made a real hash of things, haven't I?'

I squeeze her hand, but daren't say anything in case it's the wrong thing to say.

'I don't know what I thought I was doing, Bri. I guess as long as there's the smallest bit of hope, you just keep holding on. But, if I'm honest, I don't know if there's anything worth holding on to any more.'

My heart thumps inside my chest. I take a deep breath. I've never heard her speak like this before. I feel elated, excited, but scared too.

'Mum, if I got you some leaflets or something, would

you look at them? There are people you can talk to. They could help you.'

'I don't know, love,' she breathes out one long, slow, tired sigh. 'This is something Colin and I have to sort out on our own.'

I keep holding her hand. *Colin and I? Colin and I?* I want to shout: 'This isn't about you and Colin. It's about you and me. We can cut him out of our lives any time we like. We'll survive without him, you'll see.' Of course, I say nothing of the sort.

'The leaflets, it couldn't hurt to read them could it?'

Mum's eyes focus somewhere beyond the walls of this house. 'No, I don't suppose it could.'

Twenty

With the start of December the temporary break in the rain gives way to yet more downpours. Every evening the news offers festive horror stories of people flooded out of their homes and facing a damp, miserable Christmas in village halls and temporary shelters.

School feels flat, like we're all just marking time until the holidays. The mocks are over so there's no urgency any more. We don't have to hand in our course work until February so suddenly there's nothing to do. Even the teachers are feeling it. They fill up lessons with videos and discussions and you can sense that they're counting off the days till school's out, just like everyone else.

Colin's been giving me a wide berth since the sandwich incident. He knows he can't get round me any more and even Mum looks more tired these days, wary of Colin's efforts to make amends. Perhaps she's finally realised that it's all just a matter of time till the next big bust-up. But nothing else changes. You have to really *want* something to change before it actually does.

With more free time, Ian and I finally get round to calling Mr Graham and take him up on his offer of dinner. It feels a bit weird but Ian's keen and anything's preferable to a night in with Colin and Mum.

So here we are, standing outside the front door to the Graham house, a nice place on the edge of St George's Park.

'You look lovely,' Ian smiles as we wait for the door to open. 'I'm glad we made up.'

I smile at him. 'Me too.'

Mr Graham pulls open the door and there is a wash of warm, yellow light behind him. He beams when he sees us. 'Well, don't just stand there, come on in.'

The house is comfortable and bright, festooned with thick strings of tinsel and sprigs of holly. Mrs Graham appears with her hands full of baby toys and a girl I don't even recognise but know must be Amy sidles up behind her.

'It's a pleasure to finally meet you,' Mrs Graham smiles. 'Isn't it, Amy?'

'I've met them before, well, kind of,' the little girl grins. 'In the river.'

Her mother shudders. 'Don't remind me. I still have nightmares about what could have happened if Briony and Ian hadn't been there to pull you out.'

We go through to the sitting room. In the corner is a fat tree that stretches all the way up to the ceiling. Its multi-coloured lights flash away merrily, a far cry from the scene I left behind me; Colin kneeling grumpily on the floor with a tangled string of lights that stubbornly refused to flash whatever bulb he tweaked and a skinny, partially clad tree that he and Mum bought when they had their first Christmas together.

Mr Graham pops open a bottle of champagne and pours the frothing, fizzy liquid into tall thin glasses.

'Can I have one?' asks Amy and gets a good-natured scowl from both her parents.

'It's because of you we're opening this,' says her dad. 'Well, because Briony and Ian saved you.'

They are just handing round the glasses when a strangled cry sounds from a baby monitor in the corner.

'Amy's little brother,' Mrs Graham explains. 'I'll go.'

'To the pair of you.' Mr Graham raises his glass. 'Merry Christmas.'

Ian and I follow his lead. The bubbles pop against my top lip and tickle my nose. It's the first time I've ever had the real stuff.

Amy disappears and comes back a moment or two later clutching Caesar, her shaggy terrier puppy.

'And here's the true culprit, the one who started the whole fiasco,' Amy's father says.

The dog snuffles about, jumps up on Amy, and the pair of them roll around on the carpet, giggling and panting and showing off to their guests. Everything seems so relaxed and easy here.

Mr Graham smiles and shakes his head. 'Never work with children or animals.'

Later, we sit at the dining table while Amy's parents bring through steaming dishes and top up our glasses again. The champagne makes me feel light-headed. I'm scared that it'll make me do or say something I shouldn't but I feel awkward being there so I keep on sipping it.

They have made us baked salmon with asparagus, peas, sauté potatoes and a rich creamy sauce. We eat and drink and talk about school and exams and the things we want to do in the future. Ian wants to go to university to study sociology. I feel them looking at me and I reach for my glass again.

'I haven't exactly made my mind up.'

'What do you like most at school, then?' asks Mrs Graham. 'What's your best subject?'

'Briony's a scientist,' Ian butts in. 'Aren't you, Bri?'

'Well, physics is okay.' I feel embarrassed talking about myself and fidget nervously.

'Then you'll have to come out back. I've got something special to show you.'

'My dad's got a conservatory,' Amy announces proudly.

'*Ob*servatory,' corrects her mum.

'Well, it's only a telescope,' Mr Graham laughs.

'Briony's always looking up at the stars and stuff,' Ian grins.

'Well, that's because she's a physicist,' Mr Graham replies, smiling warmly at me.

Mrs G fills up my glass and I lose myself in my drink again.

'But what have stars got to do with physics?' Ian asks. 'I thought physics was just light and lenses and mirrors and all that.'

'Ah, the shortcomings of our modern school system,' sighs Mr Graham. 'Let me tell you something. The universe *is* physics, living physics. A lot of teachers seem to forget the bigger picture. They forget that what they put on the blackboard has more relevance than just the next exam. Come outside and I'll show you.'

He leads me and Ian out to the garden and towards what looks, from a distance, like an ordinary shed.

'You're going to like this,' he winks as he unlocks a giant padlock and throws back a catch. I notice that the construction is in two parts and it slides back and forward on rails.

'Push the other side back,' he instructs.

Both sides roll back to reveal not a rusty lawnmower

and a pair of shears, but a squat telescope, pointing blankly up at the sky.

'This is my 32 cm reflector telescope,' Mr Graham announces in hushed tones. 'As you can probably tell, I'm very proud of it. Don't tell my wife, but this is my *real* baby.' He pats the shiny metal drum affectionately and Ian and I exchange glances.

'So what can you see with this thing?' Ian takes a step closer.

'What d'you want to see?'

'I don't know. How about the Great Bear or whatever its name is?'

Mr Graham laughs. 'You can see that with the naked eye. We can go a little further with this machine. Remember, all the stars you see when you look up at night are part of our own, rather small, galaxy. Then you've got our neighbouring galaxies, which are actually about ten million *million* miles away. And after that you have the hundred billion or so other galaxies out there, visible only with the most sophisticated equipment.'

'I never realised we were so insignificant,' I shiver.

Mr Graham chuckles. 'I suppose that's one way of looking at it.' He bends into the telescope. 'Here, take a closer look.'

I stoop down to the eyepiece although it takes my eyes a moment or two to focus after all the champagne.

'There's no such thing as empty space,' Mr Graham continues, 'we're just restricted by how far we can see. This telescope takes us out of our own galaxy and into the neighbouring star systems. What you're looking at is over 2.2 million light years away.'

I try to quantify the distance, to visualise that immenseness stretching endlessly overhead but it just blows my mind. I have the distinct feeling of being much, much smaller than I had ever imagined.

Ian takes his turn at the telescope next, straightening back up after a moment or so. 'I mean, it's quite nice and all that, but once you've seen one star, haven't you seen them all?'

'Not at all. Some stars are changing all the time. But more importantly, this isn't just a telescope, you know. This is a *time machine*.'

Ian raises his eyebrows and throws me a glance. Mr Graham just laughs good-naturedly.

'Well, think about it. Space is so vast that it takes light a huge amount of time to cross such distances. The light coming off our neighbouring galaxy has taken about two million years to reach us. You're seeing something as it was at around the same time as when humans first walked the earth.'

Ian looks thoughtful. 'But then anything could have happened by now and you wouldn't even know about it for another two million years.'

'True.' He looks at me and shrugs. 'I see I haven't been able to convince your friend here of the merits of star-gazing. What about you?'

I bend back down for another glimpse of this hidden world far, far beyond my own. 'I think it's just incredible,' I whisper.

Mr Graham smiles. 'I thought you'd be impressed. It puts life on our planet into a rather humbling perspective, don't you think?'

I am forced to agree.

On the way home, Ian and I go via the Winterbourne shopping complex to look at the big tree in the square, which we never got to see that fateful Friday night. Ian gives my hand a squeeze and draws me up against him.

'It's romantic, don't you think?'

'Yeah, I guess.'

I know he wants me to say the things I am supposed to say, feel the things I am supposed to feel and it makes me uncomfortable because all I have inside me at the moment is a great big black hole. Still, I guess I can pretend for his sake, because, like my mum, I am good at pretending.

But something else has occurred to me tonight. It happened while I was looking up at the stars with Mr Graham, listening to, and slightly envious of, his massive enthusiasm for the universe. I've realised that instead of being a whole person, I'm more like a shell. I've spent the last few years looking out for Mum, worrying about the stuff that goes on at home and it's left me empty. I don't know what I want for my future because the present draws everything from me. I can't tell you what I'm interested in because I've never given it that much thought. It's like I don't really exist.

And then another thought strikes me: how alike we are, Mum and me. Her years with Colin have stripped her of everything she once had, once was. She doesn't know who she is any more. Take Colin away and she would probably blow away on the breeze. I shiver.

'Cold?'

'A bit.'

Ian slings his arm round me as we head off towards Lavender Avenue.

'You really get off on all that star junk, don't you?'

'Kind of,' I say. 'Yeah, I suppose I do.'

'You can put your arm round me too if you like,' he teases.

So we hug each other as we walk, just like any other couple.

'You know what a cold fish is?' he asks me presently.

'A fish that's cold?'

There's a pause.

'Something like that. You want me to come in with you?'

By this time we're standing outside my house. 'Why?'

He shrugs. 'I don't know. It's what people do, isn't it? We could have a cup of tea or something. But it's okay if you don't want me to'

'I'm very tired,' I lie. 'I think it was all that champagne.'

'Yeah, I saw you getting that down your neck. It's okay, I understand.' He has his best sympathetic expression painted on his face.

'Understand what?'

'That I can't push you too hard. It's like two steps forward and one step back with you, Bri. But that's just the way it is. I'm cool with that.'

'Look I'm tired, I just want to crash,' I feel uncomfortable again. 'You don't have to make everything into a major issue.'

Ian smiles, kisses me, taking my face in both his hands. 'I'll see you in school on Monday, then.'

'Yeah, see you.'

I watch him walking away with a sadness that gnaws at my insides. He wants more from me than I can give. Never mind 100 per cent, I don't even have 50 per cent to share with him. There just isn't enough of me to go round.

Alone in my bedroom, I draw back the curtains at my window and stare out at the night sky, at the stars millions and millions of miles above us. I try, as Mr Graham said, to get everything into some kind of perspective.

Twenty-one

The countdown to Christmas has begun. T–5 days (as they say in all the best sci-fi movies). It's Saturday morning. Me, David and Mum work round each other in the kitchen. Mum cracks eggs into the poacher and adjusts the gas. David slumps into his chair, bleary-eyed after another night of destroying his liver.

'I'll have coffee too,' he says watching Mum make some for Colin. 'Black, and strong.'

'Ah, have we got a bit of a hangover?' I yell in his ear. He swipes at me.

'You drink too much, David, you know that?' Mum clucks.

'Everyone's got to have a hobby. Mine's abusing my body,' David yawns and makes a face like a shrivelled grape.

'I hope you're not going to be in the pub all the holidays,' I scowl. 'It would be nice if you were here a bit more, wouldn't it Mum?'

'Mmm?' She's distracted by the effort of making breakfast. 'Well if David's already got plans...'

The doorbell rings and she scurries off to see who it is. I try to drown my ulcer in warm, milky tea. David catches my eye, looks away.

'So *are* you going to be around over the holidays?' I ask

him. 'You know what they can be like sometimes.'

'I only get two days off and I can do without you trying to organise my life for me, thank you very much.'

'I wasn't trying to organise your life. I just thought it might be nice for Mum.'

He drops a piece of toast onto his plate. 'God, Bri, you've always got to be poking your nose into other people's business, haven't you? Is your life so deadly dull that you've got to meddle in everyone else's, is that it?'

I mouth back at him, 'Arsehole.'

He just grins at me.

Mum comes in with a brown paper parcel in her arms. She places it on the floor, turning it over to examine the labels.

'It's from Cath – oh, and Hannah. She must be back.'

Hannah is Mum's youngest sister. She's been backpacking round the world for the last five years but, by the looks of it, she's finally hung up her hiking boots.

'Wonder what they've sent us. Shall we open it now?' I peer over Mum's shoulder.

'I expect everything will be wrapped up inside, won't it?'

'Course.' I hand her the kitchen scissors. 'You can put them round the tree. It'll be nice.'

David raises his eyebrows but doesn't say anything.

Mum cuts the string and peels away the layers of parcel tape holding it all together. Inside are several beautifully wrapped packages, all with multi-coloured paper and shiny bows.

'I must call Cath. Otherwise she'll think something's wrong. Don't let me forget, will you, Bri? My goodness, just look at all these!'

'What's this then?' Colin comes through and looks

down at her, kneeling on the floor with her precious parcels. 'A care package?'

'From Cath and Hannah.'

'Oh, the three witches back together again, then?' He smiles, half joking, half serious. 'I'd better watch out!'

Mum gets to her feet and dashes back to her poached eggs. 'Oh, I think they're still okay. Will they be too dry for you, Col, love?'

'I'll make do, I know my place,' Col sighs, reaching for his paper. 'It's always the way when your sisters hit town. No time for us, eh, Miriam?'

'Of course not,' Mum laughs breathily.

Colin opens up his news pages, folds them awkwardly. 'Sorry kids, Christmas is cancelled. Your mum's going to be spending all of her time round at her sisters'.'

The cold sun gleams outside the kitchen window. The sky is blue and cloudless. It's a perfect day for a run. Mum plops the dry poached eggs onto hot buttered toast and the four of us sit quietly around the breakfast table.

'I suppose I should start making a list for Christmas Day,' Mum says presently, breaking the silence. 'The shops are going to be packed and I have to collect the turkey today.'

'Absolutely. Christmas should be planned like a military operation,' Colin confirms from behind the pages of the *Telegraph*.

'If you give me the housekeeping, I can go this afternoon and stock up.'

He peers over the top of his paper. 'What happened to all the money I gave you last week?'

Mum's cheeks flush. 'Well, I spent it.'

Colin laughs to himself, shakes his head. 'God, woman, you're bleeding me dry here.'

'I just went to the supermarket,' Mum flounders. 'I didn't spend it on anything out of the ordinary.'

'It's what you call ordinary that worries me,' sighs Col. 'I can't win, can I?'

My stomach twinges. I glance at my mother. Although Colin appears to be joking, Mum is mortified. She watches him with big, glassy eyes as he reaches into his trouser pocket and pulls out a wad of twenties. He pads round the table to Mum and thumps them down in front of her. She jumps. We all do.

'Satisfied now?' He sits back down and picks up the paper. 'I can't keep bailing you out like this, Miriam. I'm not an endless pot that you can all take, take, take from.'

Mum just stares at the money in front of her.

When Colin and David have left the table, Mum is still sitting there, transfixed by the notes curling up at her.

'I don't ask him for much,' she whispers. 'I've never thought of him like that, Bri. I'm not that kind of person.'

'I know you're not, Mum. Don't let him get to you.'

She reaches into a kitchen drawer for a small, brown pill bottle, grapples with the cap for a moment or two, then throws a couple of tablets into her mouth.

'What are those? How long have you been popping pills?'

'I don't *pop pills*.' She washes them down with the dregs of her tea. 'These are just to steady my nerves. You know how I suffer with my nerves.'

'I know how you could *stop* suffering with your nerves.'

'Don't start, Briony. Not today. I haven't the strength.'

'So how long have you had these?' I examine the computerised label on the bottle before she snatches it from me.

'I don't know. Six months. A year. See, they're working

already. Now, why don't you help me with the shopping? We can go into town and have a look at some things for you.'

That's right, Mum – bribery, works every time.

Outside the Winterbourne shopping complex there's a brass band playing carols and Mum and I pause to listen. They're playing 'God Rest Ye Merry Gentlemen'.

'This one always makes me think of my schooldays,' Mum sighs wistfully. 'I don't know why, I suppose we must have sung it but I don't remember exactly.' She hums along with a couple of bars, lost in her own private thoughts. 'So, Briony, have you thought about what you want, love?'

I shrug. 'I don't know. Nothing special.'

We've been trawling the shops looking for stuff that David might like. We settle on a couple of tops and some CDs. As we head down King Street we pass a mobile phone shop. As usual, it's packed with people. I slow down.

'What about a mobile phone?'

Mum looks alarmed. 'They cost a fortune.'

'No they don't. Not any more. All my friends have one.'

'A mobile phone? Oh, I don't know.' Mum allows herself to be dragged back to the shop window.

'The thing is, it could be useful. I mean, since the house phone got broken and...' I falter, unsure of how to word what I want to say, 'well, if Colin did anything and you needed to phone someone, I mean in an emergency...'

I expect Mum to resist, to pretend she doesn't know what I'm talking about, but surprisingly enough she just nods, like she's almost considering it. Her eyes skate over the mass of bodies stuffed inside the shop.

'Well, maybe I'll come back when it's not so busy,' she says and leaves it at that.

With the shopping done, I'm free to escape to my own private world. I go home, change and go running. The air feels thin as I storm up to the park. People are out in their hats and scarves, walking dogs and pushing prams, their faces full of festive cheer. They just look stupid to me.

I think about phoning Ian. I also think about just letting things slide between us but I'm scared that he'll call round again if I do that. I can see him now, beaming innocently and trying to make casual chit-chat with my mum, while Colin fumes silently in the background.

Things have been cooler between us since that night at the Grahams. I try to convince myself that I'm imagining it, but Ian hangs back from making the first move now, doesn't peck me on the cheek between classes or anything. It's as if he's waiting for me to take the initiative, to show him it's a two-way street, I suppose.

I push myself faster, trying to get rid of this muddle of feelings. More than anything I want to be wrapped up in that lovely warm glow of a steady relationship, like Lisa and Steve, but I know that it won't change the things that are wrong deep down inside me. I feel like I'm being dishonest, playing games with Ian, going through my lines, but I don't know what else to do. I *do* still fancy him. And I *don't* want to hurt him. Perhaps that's enough for now.

Later that afternoon, I run down to the phone box on the corner and call him. We arrange to meet back at St George's Park. When he arrives, I present him with the Christmas card I have been carrying around in my bag for the last two weeks, unsure whether to give it to him or not.

'This is for you. I wasn't going to buy into the whole commercial, sentimental Christmas thing, but hey, I guess I'm weakening. What can I say?'

I watch his face as he opens the pink envelope and reads the card. The words on it declare: 'For Someone Really Special'.

'It's great, Bri.' I get a kiss and some kids wolf-whistle as they whiz past on their bikes. 'I got you something too. I wasn't going to give it to you, I mean, I know what you think about Christmas and everything, but well...' He reaches inside his jacket and pulls out a bright turquoise envelope. 'Happy Christmas anyway.'

On this card there are two teddy bears holding paws and walking through the snow. It reads 'To My Girlfriend'. Sappy, but hell, that's what Christmas is all about. When I look up at him he's grinning at me with that big froggy mouth of his.

'D'you want to go to the Corn Exchange? Steve and Lisa are heading down there, I think. So are Francine and Aysha.'

'Sure, yeah, whatever,' I shrug, smiling weakly. 'It sounds nice.'

So we head off into the rain, jackets over our heads, running through the puddles like the love-struck teenagers the great play requires.

Twenty-two

T–2. Colin is off work now and is up bright and early washing the car and humming carols to himself. When he's finished, he takes Mum out for some 'last-minute shopping' and leaves me in front of the TV watching some slushy, feel-good movie.

Once I have the house to myself I switch on the computer and log on to the Internet once more. I'm curious to see how the likes of Goldie and Angel will be spending their holidays. There are new names beside theirs on the message board, but, sadly, the stories are all still the same. No Christmas cheer there.

Colin and Mum waltz back into the house two or three hours later, bent under the weight of bags and boxes, chattering away merrily.

'There's more in the car, love, if you want to make yourself useful,' Col announces as I slouch through the doorway.

I watch them stocking the fridge and the kitchen cupboards with food and booze. There are some bags pushed to one side that clearly don't contain food, with rolls of fancy wrapping paper sticking out the top.

'Right, I think I shall retire to the bedroom and get this little lot wrapped before anyone's tempted to take a peek,' smiles Col.

He nuzzles affectionately at Mum's neck as he passes her. Her face is flushed and sparkling.

'Col's in a good mood,' I note once he is safely out of earshot.

Mum is humming her way round the kitchen.

'And why shouldn't he be? It *is* Christmas in case you've forgotten, Briony, a time of goodwill and cheer. You could do with a bit of that yourself.'

'Yeah, but what about all the other stuff?' My voice sounds like a sullen little schoolgirl. 'You're not going to just forget about everything else are you?'

Mum stifles a sigh.

'Did you read that stuff I gave you?' I persist.

'Bri!' she exhales sharply.

'What? I'm only asking.'

'Now's hardly the time, is it?' She glances anxiously at the hallway.

'It's never the right time, though, is it, Mum?'

She looks away, but then surprises me. 'Yes, Briony. I did look at it.'

'And?'

'And what?' She turns back. 'What d'you expect me to do, love?'

'You could talk to someone. That Domestic Violence Liaison Officer perhaps.'

Mum hisses for me to be quiet. 'I don't like talking to people. It's private, between me and Colin. I don't want strangers coming in and making judgements on what a rotten wife and mother I've been.'

'That's not what they're there for, Mum. I just want you to *do* something before it gets really out of hand. I don't want you getting hurt any more.'

'And you think what you're suggesting isn't going to

hurt?' she says softly. 'You think it's that easy just to turn my back on everything?'

Now it's my turn to look away. I hadn't thought of it like that.

'I know what you think, Briony. You think I should leave. You think I should have left months ago. But you can't just switch off your feelings like that. You keep hoping that things will get better, that the person you fell in love with will come back. You think you can *make* him come back, so you hang on, and hope. I'm not sure that I'm ready to give up on him yet.'

'Yeah, but what you said before, after he broke the photo...'

'I was upset, we'd just had a fight.'

'So now you're back to wishing it all away? Closing your eyes and pretending nothing's wrong?' I whisper urgently.

My mother shakes her head. 'Look, Briony, I don't have all the answers. Let's just try to have a nice Christmas, okay?'

I give in. I feel like the Spirit of Christmas Past, spreading doom and gloom over everything I touch.

Twenty-three

Christmas Eve. T–1. Colin's been putting up shelves, has touched up the walls in the dining room, fixed the shower head in the main bathroom and even mended the hoover, and all (as far as I can tell) without so much as a hint of a cross word or sarcastic comment. Maybe there's something magical to Christmas after all.

In the evening he takes over the kitchen, making mulled wine and filling the house with spicy scents while Mum and I sit in front of the telly and watch the lights on the tree flash on off, on off, on off.

'So, did you remember to phone Aunty Cath?'

Mum nods, reaches into the Quality Street drum without taking her eyes from the TV screen.

'And what did she say? Did you speak to Hannah?'

'I did. They both send their best.' She keeps her voice low, presumably so Colin won't hear her.

'And?'

'Cath said we should all get together some time. I can't think of the last time I saw Hannah. I said maybe after the holidays, said I'd call her.'

'That'll make Colin happy,' I grimace.

Mum just stuffs a sweet into her mouth.

Colin comes through with a tray of steaming mugs

and a smug look on his face.

'So, who's for mulled wine?' he beams.

We take our drinks and he waits like an expectant schoolboy.

It's too hot to drink straight off. An earthy smell fills my nostrils as I breathe into the spicy steam. Mum sips at it.

'Ooh, it's a little sharp, Col, love.'

Colin frowns, obviously not expecting to encounter criticism after his unprecedented effort. He takes a scalding gulp from his own cup.

'Perhaps it could use just a little extra sugar,' Mum offers.

'Yeah, well, I should have known it wouldn't be quite right for you, Miriam,' he grunts sourly. 'Don't know why I even bother trying.'

The hairs down my back prickle.

'No, it's lovely, Col.' Mum takes a second sip to appease him. 'Really nice.'

'But a little *tart*,' he remarks pointedly. 'Perhaps it's all those chocolates you've been stuffing into that fat face of yours.'

And with that he takes his tray back out to the kitchen where he sits and broods, darkly. Mum keeps her eyes fixed on the TV, one hand dangling in the sweetie tin, toying distractedly with the chocolates.

Later that night I come downstairs to get a drink of water and catch them both dancing round the living room to the music from the television, any bad feelings well and truly buried, forgotten. Their bodies are pressed tightly into one another, eyes closed, swaying and turning in time with the music. You'd think they didn't have a care in the world. I crouch on the stairs, watching them, wondering about things, and suddenly I feel very, very lonely.

Christmas Day. Carols on the radio as Mum fixes breakfast, singing along to herself, happy because, for one day at least, the fairy tale and the reality merge seamlessly together. The vegetables are already peeled and sitting in pans of water, ready to go. Mum glances at the clock on the wall. Colin is right. Christmas has to be planned like a military operation.

Even David is on his best behaviour this morning. After breakfast we go through to the living room and open each other's presents.

'What time is it?' he whines.

'Don't you dare think about going to the pub, not today, David. Not Christmas Day.'

'Your mum's right,' says Colin in one of his rare shows of parental solidarity. 'Today's a day for families.'

'I just want to see what's on telly.' David reaches for the TV guide, obviously resigned to spending the day indoors.

'You better hope someone's given you a watch, then,' smirks Colin. 'If, of course, you've ever learned to tell the time, that is. I've seen no evidence of it myself.'

David scowls and reaches for one of the presents under the tree.

'Here, Bri, you might as well open mine first.' He hands me a book-shaped parcel.

As I rip off the paper I see that it is indeed a book. A guide to astronomy. I stare gob-smacked at this gift from my otherwise distant and most definitely alien brother.

'But how did you know?'

He shrugs. 'Mum said you were into all that stuff. I just found it in a bookshop.'

I am speechless that my brother David, who has drifted steadily further and further away from me over the last few years, should have bought me something so special.

'Thanks, David, that's really excellent.'

His face actually goes a little pink.

Colin gives both me and Mum jewellery. I unwrap the small package determined to hate it but inside there's a beautiful silver necklace with some kind of small, sea-blue stone dangling from it.

'It's lovely,' I breathe, more surprised than anything.

'Oh, Colin, love, you shouldn't have,' exclaims Mum as she opens her box and finds a gold and emerald chain together with matching earrings. 'This is far too good for me.'

'Nonsense.' Colin helps her fasten the clasp around the back of her neck and kisses her softly.

'But when would I wear it?' Mum gasps.

Colin frowns. 'If you don't like it, I can take it back.'

'But I love it!'

My stomach twangs.

Col's brother, his only living relative from what I can make out, has sent him a bottle of something, just as he does every Christmas. Colin tears at the store's gift wrapping, shaking his head all the while. He pulls out a bottle of whisky.

'God, fifty years old and he still can't choose a decent Scotch,' he mutters, setting it down beside his armchair. 'Right, what's next?'

The biggest surprise of all is from Mum. She has bought me a mobile phone and a set of pre-paid vouchers to get me started.

'All her friends have them,' she tells Colin as I programme the settings the way I want them. 'At least this way she can pay for her own phone calls to her boyfriend.'

I glance at the pair of them. Have they forgotten that the house phone hasn't worked since Colin smashed it over her head? They're as bad as each other.

'So you're having a relationship with that yob now?' Colin enquires.

'I wouldn't say that exactly.' I punch the buttons on my phone. 'We're friends. We go out occasionally. That's all.'

'This is an important year for you,' he lectures. 'We don't want you getting distracted by the likes of boyfriends and whatnot.'

I glance up at him as Mum goes to check on the turkey. He gave up his rights to give me fatherly advice the first time he slapped my mother. But Colin is a law unto himself.

The smell of turkey filters through the house as Mum clatters the pots and pans amidst great clouds of steam. Both David and I play our part, taking the dishes through to the dining room. Even Colin is attempting to lend a hand, carrying through the mat which Mum uses to stand really hot stuff on so that it doesn't mark the table.

'I think we're ready for the turkey,' he announces, reaching into the fridge for a chilled bottle of wine.

'Well, let's all sit down then.' Mum sounds as if she can't believe how smoothly things have gone today.

The three of us take our places at the dining-room table. Moments later, Mum marches proudly in with the turkey tray in her oven-gloved hands. She looks hot but happy. Her eyes search for the mat on the table.

'Col, love, where's the mat?'

Colin sits in his chair at the head of the table and takes a long, slow sip of wine, pretending not to have heard her.

'Col?' The turkey is heavy in her hands. 'The mat, Colin, love?' Her voice wavers.

Colin continues to sit where he is, eyes fixed dead ahead, blanking her.

I can see Mum's chest heaving in and out as it slowly dawns on her that he is playing one of his little games again. She looks about her desperately.

'Col? This tray's ever so hot, love.'

She goes to put the tray down on one of the place mats and he looks accusingly at her.

'Don't do that, Miriam; it'll mark the wood.'

His words defy her to go against him even though the heat from the turkey tray is burning through her old gloves. I feel sick.

'But it's hot, love,' Mum whimpers.

'Where are you going?' he barks as she turns to go back to the kitchen.

'The tray's burning my hands.'

'Then put it down.'

Mum just stands there, with this stupid great turkey, unable to do anything. She knows she can't win. She marks the table and he beats her. She doesn't put it on the table and it burns her hands. She stares at him as if she can't quite believe this is happening after everything has gone so well.

After what seems like five of the longest seconds in history, Colin, still without looking at anyone, gets slowly to his feet, reaches over to the sideboard and miraculously pulls the missing mat out of a drawer. He places it on the table and Mum almost drops the turkey onto it. Still without saying a word, Colin gently pulls off her oven gloves and examines her hands in his own giant shovels. Across her delicate pink palms are deep red blotches. He looks at them, then kisses the burns softly. Mum's eyes glass over.

'Now, let's sit down and eat,' he whispers and Mum, as if under some hypnotic spell falls into her seat, still in her apron and watches silently as Colin slowly carves the turkey.

Not another word is spoken throughout the meal. And the crackers remain unpulled as we sit in front of our puddings, forcing it all down our throats in great choking lumps.

Twenty-four

Sometimes it's the small things that make the greatest difference. Like the incident with the turkey. I could see from Mum's face that it hurt her far more than any casual backhander, perhaps because it was not done in anger. This was a malicious, pre-planned act, designed quite simply to hurt her. It chipped another little bit out of her protective armour.

It's now Boxing Day and Colin is sat in front of the TV, making a sizeable dent in his brother's inferior whisky. Mum is doing the breakfast dishes, the washing, going through the motions of every other day. I stay out of the way as much as I can, lie on my bed and look at the mobile phone in my hand. I think about calling Ian and Lisa, tap in their numbers, store them safely away in the phone book but for some reason never actually press 'call'. I'm not sure what I would say anyway. Don't want to bring the outside world rushing back in on me so soon.

David slips out of the house at lunch-time, probably to get re-acquainted with his bar stool at the Prince of Wales. I continue to lie on my bed, watching the sky grow darker as the afternoon light fades behind more rain clouds and night draws in on us.

'Can I interest you in a turkey sandwich?' Mum pokes

her head round my bedroom door.

'Yeah, whatever. I'm not really fussed.'

'You've got to eat something. You didn't touch your lunch.'

'I've got stomach ache.'

'It's probably all those sweets. Take some bicarb. I expect it's just a touch of indigestion. I'll lay the table anyway.'

I slope downstairs as Mum fries up some of the vegetables left over from yesterday's unforgettable feast.

'You okay, Mum?'

She looks round. 'I expect I'll live, Briony. I always have before.'

'You look tired.'

'Yes, I am feeling a bit tired,' she nods.

Colin comes in, weaving a somewhat crooked path round the table in order to get to the fridge.

'Tired? What do you do to tire you out?' He leans on the fridge door, letting out a blast of icy air as his red eyes search lazily for something to snack on. 'It's not as if you work. It's not as if you have anything to do.'

'Except the cooking and the cleaning and everything else that comes with running a house,' Mum sighs.

My stepfather turns, leans back into the fridge, the door still wide open. He forces his eyes to focus on my mother. It takes a couple of seconds.

'I beg your pardon?' He rocks backwards a little. 'You're never happy are you, Miriam? You're a miserable cow these days, d'you know that?' He stumbles forwards and shuts the fridge door. 'Tired! Tired my arse!' he mumbles. 'Why don't you just say what you really mean? That you're tired of me. That's right, isn't it? That's what you really want to say. Tired of me!'

His eyes follow Mum as she switches off the gas under the frying pan and scrapes the vegetables onto three plates. My breath catches like razor blades in my throat.

'Yes, Col. I'm tired. Tired of the way that everything always ends in a fight these days. I just can't keep doing this any more.'

I can't believe what I'm seeing. She's finally saying something to that pathetic excuse for a man, after all these agonising months. She's finally done it. My heart pounds.

It takes a few more seconds for Colin's whisky-soaked brain to process her words. I watch his face as it searches for an expression. He takes a couple of drunken steps towards her but she just pushes him away, like swatting away an irritating fly.

'You stink of booze,' she says with contempt, refusing to look him in the face.

Colin raises his hand as if he's going to slap her. She flinches but stands her ground.

'No more. This can't go on. *We* can't go on like this, Colin.' She turns to face him. 'I mean it, Colin. I can't do this any more.'

His hand is there in mid-air, ready to strike but temporarily paralysed by this unprecedented display of defiance.

'Who do you think you are to be telling me what to do?' he slurs. His raised hand becomes a pointing finger, jabbed into Mum's face.

'I'm your wife, Colin.' She turns away.

'Yeah. *My* wife. *Mine.* You do as I say, not the other way around, you ungrateful little cow.'

Mum edges away from him, picks off the cold slices of turkey from under the tinfoiled carcass sitting on the counter. Colin watches in drunken disbelief.

'Don't you dare ignore me, you bitch!' he hollers and blindly reaches for the frying pan, smashing it down on the edge of the work surface. Spots of hot fat fly into the air, prick at my face. The pan clangs to the floor and Mum gasps. Colin's chest heaves under his new Christmas pullover.

'So what are you going to do, eh?' Colin bellows, his voice getting louder. 'What are you going to do if you're so damn unhappy, if I've made your life so bloody miserable? Leave?'

The question hangs for a moment in the air. I feel dizzy waiting for Mum's reply. My knees shake. I want her to say yes but I'm scared of what he'll do if she does.

'You need help,' Mum mutters quietly.

'*I* need help? *I* need help?' Colin screeches, swaying backwards into the cupboard. 'Are you sure about that, Miriam?'

There is a look of such absolute hatred on his face now that it turns my blood into liquid nitrogen. He lets out this pained cry, wheels around and, with an outstretched arm, sweeps everything off the counter behind him. Plates and vegetables bounce to the floor. Cutlery pings after it. Then his eyes alight on the knife block in the far corner. At the same time both Mum and I are instantly aware of it too.

'Oh, no, Colin, don't be stupid, love.'

He pulls out a vegetable knife, one with a big fat blade and stands there admiring it and chuckling slightly to himself as he touches the edge gently with his thumb.

Colin has centre stage once more, all eyes fixed on him and the knife. Mum takes a step backwards, the balance of power once more against her.

'You can't be serious. Don't, love.'

I feel tears rising inside me, don't know whether to go towards my mum or back out of the room. I have a mobile phone now. I could call for help. But helping usually makes things worse. I can't afford to make this worse, not when he's got a knife in his stupid, drunken hands.

'This has gone far enough, Colin.' Mum's voice wavers, giving her away.

Her fear makes his whisky smile wider. He makes a huge show of putting the knife back in its block, then takes a couple of steps towards her. Mum backs up against the work surface. Her face wrinkles as she feels his breath on her.

'I don't really think you're the one to be telling me what to do, Miriam, do you?' he asks, his face leering at her.

'I'm warning you.' Her voice cracks.

'No, I don't think so,' he laughs.

'Briony, go and call the police!'

Our eyes lock together. I falter, momentarily unsure. My legs are like lollipop sticks, I don't think that they will be able to carry me that far.

'Briony's not going anywhere,' Colin announces. 'Briony's going to watch while I give her lousy excuse for a mother a good hiding.'

His words snap me out of my daydream. I bolt for the door but Colin calls me back.

'Are you really sure you want to do that? You go anywhere and you'll only make it worse for your dear mother,' Colin's face flinches spasmodically, 'and it'll all be your fault.'

At this, my mother bursts into life with a sudden sobbing sound deep in the back of her throat. 'No, Colin! No more!' Her arms flail against him, no longer caring what he does to her. She's like a demented windmill, slapping and hitting at him blindly, anything to get away from him.

Her attack throws him off guard, and off balance. He stumbles backwards, but as Mum comes at him again, he punches her hard in the stomach. She doubles over, gasping and choking for breath. Seizing his chance, and always the big man who's not afraid to kick someone when they're down, he follows this up with a succession of vicious blows to whatever part of her body he can make contact with, one after another, again and again, then tops it off by bringing his knee sharply into her face. I can almost hear the crack as her whole head jars backwards. She crumples into a heap on the floor.

'Leave her alone!' I scream as Colin takes a step towards her.

He stares at me with those wild red eyes of his and somehow it roots me to the spot. Colin swears drunkenly, dismissively, then turns his attention back to my mother.

'You think I like being like this?' he yells.

Mum's head is drooping into her chest and she can barely keep herself sitting upright.

'You think this is fun for me? You *make* me do it, Miriam. I know what you say about me behind my back.'

'I don't say anything.' Her eyelids slide shut.

'No? Not even to your sisters?'

'I haven't spoken to them in ages.'

Colin laughs. 'Well, you see that kind of proves my point, doesn't it? Because now I know you're lying. I *saw* you, Miriam. In the phone box, not a week ago.'

Mum's face flickers. She pulls herself away, guiltily, as if suddenly this really is all her fault. Her head lolls against her chest and she sags a little further into the floor. I edge cautiously over to her, try to pull her up but she cries out in pain. Colin just stands there, swaying over the pair of us.

'After all I've done for you,' he slurs. 'This is how you repay me.'

'You've done nothing for her!' My heart aches in my chest. I look up at him, almost willing him to start on me. I think I am finally angry enough to tear him a new face.

'The only thing you've ever done is belittle her and beat her down again and again. You've done nothing for any of us!'

'Briony. Leave it,' Mum hisses a warning to me, eyes closed against the pain.

'No, let her speak,' Colin says in his sing-song, playful voice. 'Let her get it off her chest. She's obviously *dying* to say something.'

But I can't speak. And in that instant I hate him more than I've ever hated him before. He sees it in my face but all he does is laugh.

'No, that's what I thought.'

I am determined not to show Colin how scared I am but my whole body is trembling. I feel vulnerable kneeling down beside my mother, aware of this dark, drunken shape looming over us. I look at Mum's crumpled body, figuring out how to get her upright again, silently willing her to help me. Come on Mum, get up. Don't let him do this to you. She takes small, hurt breaths. I turn on my stepfather, masking fear with absolute hatred and two years of pent-up anger.

'I hate you! Look what you've done to her!' I scream. 'I hate you!'

He looks but doesn't see. I hold her battered, bruised face up to show him. He lurches forward and grabs Mum roughly by her elbow, attempting to yank her onto her feet. She gags with the pain.

'Stop making a show of yourself, Miriam. Go and clean yourself up.'

Blindly, Mum gropes her way to the sink and splashes cold water over herself but she's still holding herself strangely. Hurting.

'She needs a doctor.'

'She's fine.'

'She can't even stand up straight.'

Colin looks her up and down.

'She needs to see a doctor,' I say again.

'She'll be okay.' But there's a trace of uncertainty creeping into his voice.

'No, Colin, it really hurts,' Mum gasps, holding her side.

He wipes his giant paws over his face a couple of times.

'It's okay, Mum, we can get you a taxi to the hospital.' I push past Colin and gently take her elbow, steadying her, squeezing her, scared to let go in case her resolve falters and she slopes off to bed to lick her wounds, the way she normally does.

Suddenly it's screamingly clear what I must do. I need to get her out of this house. If I can get her away from here, then maybe we will all have a chance. I can't let her give in to him again. Not now.

'She's not taking a sodding taxi.' Colin growls. 'She can't go out looking like that.'

I am desperate. I feel that our whole future is somehow dependent on what happens in the next few minutes. I look at her again but already her eyes are slowly dying.

Twenty-five

Colin glares at me and Mum. He puffs and blows, wondering what to do next. Mum starts to droop and I squeeze harder at her arm.

'I'll get you to hospital, Mum,' I mutter as she rests her head on my shoulder.

'It hurts.'

'She's not getting a taxi,' Colin spits.

'Well, how else is she going to get there? She can hardly bloody walk, can she?'

'Okay, I'll drive her.'

'You can't. You've been drinking.' My heart leaps. I don't want him there.

'I'm not letting her out in a taxi for all and sundry to see,' Colin shouts. 'I said I'll drive, so I'll bloody well drive you.'

There's nothing I can do. He's too drunk to drive, but we have no choice. If I push too hard, he may well put his foot down and forbid Mum to leave the house all together. He might even start on her again. I edge my mum away from the kitchen cupboards and help her into the hall where she insists on putting on her jacket before she will go out. She can only get one arm in so I pull the rest of it up over her shoulder. My stepfather stumbles out to the garage to warm up the car and clear his head.

'Be strong, Mum. You can do this. It'll be all right,' I whisper.

She takes heavy steps to the front door, almost as if she doesn't really want to go. Perhaps she knows that everything could change once she steps over the threshold. I hold her tightly, propelling her forwards. I am scared to breathe too deeply, to upset anything, to stop this from happening. I even find myself mimicking her shallow, painful breaths.

Maybe we are lucky that there is so little traffic on the roads as it makes Colin's job of driving us much easier. Not that he seems drunk any more. He is sombre and has a fixed expression on his face, eyes squinting determinedly through the windscreen.

'We should have left a note for David,' my mother says distantly. 'What if he comes home and finds we're all out?'

'He's got a key. He'll be all right.'

'Okay, let's get things straight,' my stepfather interrupts. 'We were clearing out the loft when you pulled a tea chest down on top of yourself.' He glances across at my mother to see whether she is taking in his cover story. 'You were in the loft when a tea chest fell on you. Okay, Miriam? There's no point in making this any worse than it has to be.'

I wonder what he means by that.

'We can work this out by ourselves, can't we? We always did before. What do you say? Miriam?'

For the first time that I can remember, he sounds really anxious.

My mother nods slightly, mutters something, but continues staring out of her window at the streets and houses floating by.

'Where is this bloody hospital anyway?' Colin swerves down a road on the left, clipping the kerb and throwing my mother against the door.

She whimpers slightly. He looks over at her.

'We'll be there in a jiffy, Miriam. It'll be okay, you'll see. I'll make things better for you, just like I always do.'

As we pull into the carpark I give Mum's shoulder a squeeze from the back seat, just to let her know that I'm still here. Colin falls out of the car and opens Mum's door for her, then eases her out, steadying her or steadying himself, who can tell? I want to push him aside. *I* want to look after her. He has no right to be concerned about her. I tag along behind them as they make their crooked way towards the accident and emergency department.

Colin is like an octopus, his arms protectively smothering my mother, shielding her from me and everyone else. He follows the signs to a side room where a male nurse is checking people in, assessing their injuries.

'A tea chest fell on top of her as we were clearing out some of the rubbish from our loft,' he explains as the nurse motions for Mum to take a seat.

He doesn't seem to hear Colin, asks Mum for her name, shines a light in her eyes, asks *her* if she can tell him what happened.

'Just a stupid accident,' Mum breathes.

'Didn't you hear what I said?' Col demands. 'We were clearing out the loft.'

The nurse glances up just briefly before writing something on to a piece of paper. He asks Mum where it hurts most. She indicates her side and attempts to pull up her top for him to see. Colin drops to his knees beside her and clumsily lifts the sweater for her. He rubs her hand gently.

'Can't you give her something for the pain?'

'Not until a doctor's seen her, I'm afraid.' He gives us a card with her details on.

'And how long will that be?'

'For non-serious cases there's a waiting time of about fifty minutes at present.'

'Oh, is that what she is? A non-serious case?' Colin retorts irritably.

'Technically, yes. If you'll just take a seat, someone will call you as soon as they can.'

My stepfather doesn't argue his point. He sees that the nurse will not bend the rules just to suit him. I wonder if the nurse can smell the alcohol on Colin's breath; if he's already clocked his bloodshot eyes. Col hands Mum's registration card to me, lifts my mother to her feet and escorts her back to the waiting area – a large, shabby white room with rows of uncomfortable wooden benches and a bright red Coke machine. Colin sits with his arm round my mother's shoulder, patting her hand. He makes me sick, the way he's pretending all of this isn't his fault.

On one wall is a flashing red display which keeps us informed of waiting times. Mum sits quietly in her seat next to Colin, who is now drunkenly stroking her hair. He whispers things to her softly, brainwashing her, making things better before the doctor has a chance to intervene.

After about thirty minutes he can sit still no longer and goes off to get Mum and himself a drink of water, stalking back to the nurse in the side room to double-check that there is absolutely no possibility of him speeding things up for us. I shuffle over to my Mum.

'You okay there?'

'I can't breathe properly. I've got this stabbing pain in my side.'

'I think maybe he's busted your ribs. What are you going to tell the doctors?'

Mum turns to look at me and shakes her head. I stare down at the scuffed grey vinyl beneath my feet and feel every last bit of energy draining out of me. By the time Mum's name is finally called I can barely lift myself off the seat.

'Are you all together?' the lady asks. 'Perhaps you two would like to wait over there while the doctor's with her?'

She nods towards another smaller waiting area. I wonder if this is procedure, or if they know something is wrong. What do they see when they look at my stepfather, I wonder? Can they piece together all the bits of our family jigsaw, or do they only see what Colin allows them to see? I stare at the nurse, hoping that she can read my mind but she just smiles a kind, professional smile and helps Mum onto a bed inside a cubicle.

'Miriam?'

'I'll be fine. I'll call you if I need anything.'

The nurse draws the curtain as a young doctor saunters up. My stepfather and I are forced to wait for their verdict.

Say something Mum, I will her, *say something for God's sake. This could be the beginning of the rest of your life.*

The curtain swishes all the way back and the nurse summons us over. My mother is now wearing one of those blue cotton hospital gowns. She looks anxious.

'They want me to stay in overnight.'

My stepfather takes her hand in his and turns to the nurse for some kind of explanation.

'She has extensive bruising to the face and chest and two broken ribs.'

'And you think she needs to stay in overnight? I mean, I'm still on holiday, I could easily look after her if it's just a bit of rest she needs.'

The nurse looks back at him with that professional mask of hers. 'Under the circumstances, the doctor felt it would be wise to keep her in.'

Colin nods as if he understands. Under the circumstances. What does that mean? Did she speak to them? I scan her face for answers but all I see is pain and painkillers all mushed up together.

'Well, yes, of course, if you think that's best.' Colin's voice betrays his own anxiety.

The nurse nods, smiles, says something to my mother then leaves.

'I'll be fine,' Mum laughs, wearing her own mask once more. 'You two go home, there's nothing else you can do here.'

'We'll bring you some night clothes, some of your things,' offers Col.

'I'll only be in for one night. I'll be all right, love.' Mum sounds oddly determined. 'I don't want either of you worrying about me. And there's no point you going home and then coming straight back again.'

'I don't understand why they want you to stay in though,' says Col desperately.

Because you've beaten her halfway senseless, you stupid, stupid bastard, I scream silently.

'Are you sure you wouldn't rather come home, Mimi? Briony and I can look after you.'

Mimi? He hasn't called her that since they were first married. He really is running scared.

'I don't want to go against the doctor's advice.'

'Yes, but, Miriam, hospitals today, you know what they're like. You'll spend the night on a trolley and go home with more bugs than you came in with.'

Mum laughs a little. I think the drugs are finally kicking in.

'Do they know we've got insurance? We'll get you a private room at least.'

'Well, the nurse is coming. You can tell her,' Mum says sleepily. 'I think right now I could sleep anywhere.'

Twenty-six

It feels weird being alone in the car with Colin. I realise how rare it is for the two of us to be together, one on one. I sit in the front seat staring straight ahead at the road, concentrating on not seeing anything, taking shallow breaths so that I don't need to smell his stale air.

'You know I never meant for this to happen,' Colin says. 'I never meant to hurt your mother.'

I don't answer. Whether he means it or not is irrelevant. The fact is he does it. He thumps Mum and then Mum makes excuses for him. I don't suppose either of them actually *mean* for it to happen. It's just another of those laws of physics, like $E=MC^2$.

I shift my gaze to the inky black sky. It's a clear night and the stars are out in force, burning distantly and beautifully as they have done for thousands of years and will continue doing until they've used up all their fuel and there's nothing left for them to burn, no sparkle left. After that they fade into cold, hard lumps of matter or die out in a massive explosion that scatters debris across the universe in all directions. New stars are formed from the fall-out and the whole cycle can start over again. Everything goes in cycles. A never-ending cycle. Life and death and the whole messy bit in between.

The house feels cold without my mother scurrying through it. I can't remember the last time I came home to find she wasn't here. She's chained to this place – her nice neat house with everything *just so*. Trapped in it night and day.

Some time before ten David slinks home and bounces round the kitchen, looking for a sandwich, unable to work out where they come from or how to get them, completely dependent on our mother for food.

'Aren't you even going to ask where Mum is?' I growl at him.

'I thought she was upstairs.'

'She's in hospital.'

He flinches a little, bangs cupboard drawers in his quest for a sandwich filling. 'What's she doing there?'

'What d'you bloody think? They had an argument, didn't they?'

'Is she going to be okay?'

'Oh, sure. Just fine,' I snort sarcastically.

David looks at me. 'Don't take it out on me, Bri. I didn't bloody put her there.'

'So that makes it none of your business, I suppose?'

My brother swears under his breath. 'Yeah, well what would you like me to do about it, eh? What do you think I can do about it? What can *any* of us do about it, come to that? This is her bloody mess, she made her choice, Bri. It's her bloody life.'

I shake my head. It could be her death too, if she doesn't do something about it soon, but David is like an ostrich, head firmly wedged in the sand. I hate him yet envy him at the same time.

I go upstairs and lie on my bed, listening to the faint sounds of the TV from the sitting room. I feel so completely alone. How can Colin live with himself? It's as if he doesn't even recognise what he's done. He's always like that – it's always somebody's else's fault, never his own.

I get out my mobile and toy with the idea of calling Lisa but I can't face playing the funny best friend. Can't bear the thought of listening to how happy she and Steve are when my life is so crap.

It's late now and Colin has gone to bed. I sneak downstairs and log on to the Internet.

```
Subject: Secrets
From: Briony
Hello everyone. I've read your
messages before but never actually
posted one myself — until now. I just
feel that if I don't talk to someone
soon I'll go mad. The problem is my
stepfather. He beats my mother. Today
she ended up in hospital. He calls her
useless and stupid but then after a
big fight he'll tell her how sorry he
is and somehow everything is
forgotten. I'm scared for my mum
because she never seems to learn. I'm
scared what will happen to her if I'm
not around to help. But then I get
angry because I don't want to spend my
whole life looking out for her. Angry
```

> because I can't just be a normal
> teenager and have friends round to the
> house or go out for a night on the
> town. I suppose that makes me a really
> selfish person, doesn't it?

Saturday morning. Colin is up early and there's toast and coffee made when I stumble downstairs after a night of tossing and turning. My eyes ache and my belly burns as if I've been drinking paint stripper. Col pours me a coffee and I stare at it, too tired to tell him that I don't even drink the stuff.

'We'll visit your mum early,' he tells me. 'Take her a big bunch of flowers; something to cheer her up.'

He has his Blitz spirit on, his wartime good humour.

I take a piece of toast from his carefully constructed pile of cooling slices and it collapses like a house of cards. I don't care if he shouts at me. Not that he will when he's in one of these brave-faced moods. Make do and mend. That's what they used to tell people during the war. We did something about it in history. Make do and mend. That's what he's doing now. Trying to mend the things he's broken. Like my mother. She'll come home and he'll fuss over her for a couple of days and promise her that nothing like this is ever going to happen again and she'll be too tired or too dazed to do anything else but believe him.

I can't wait to be out of this house. Not just running, but for good, college or something – anything to get out of here. But then I think about Mum and wonder what will happen to her if I'm not around. I can't imagine leaving her, however much I hate this place. As always I'm torn in two, ripped right down the middle.

*

On the way to the hospital we stop at traffic lights and there's a guy selling flowers along the central reservation. Colin waves him over. He selects bunch after bunch, about four lots. The lights change and he's still hunting for change in his trouser pockets. The car behind him beeps its horn and I hang my head a bit lower, wishing I was somewhere else.

'Oh, take the bloody lot.' Colin pushes a crumpled roll of notes into the guy's hand. 'It's only money after all.'

The flower-seller laughs and shakes his head.

'Cheers, mate!' He waves after our car as it purrs off through the busy crossroads.

I expect he thinks it's Christmas, I muse, before realising that it actually is.

'Oh, I wish someone would buy me flowers like that!' one of the nurses swoons as we enter the ward.

'I'm sure they do,' Colin smiles benignly from behind his foliage. 'All lovely ladies deserve flowers.'

She giggles. 'Try telling my boyfriend that. I think you're part of a dying breed.'

God, I'm going to puke.

'I just thought they'd cheer her up,' says Colin the Good.

'They'd certainly cheer me up!' the innocent nurse drools. 'You've got visitors, Mrs Bliss, and just look what they've brought for you.'

For a brief second I see my mother without her mask. Then, forcing herself upright in her bed, she rearranges her face and her expression is back to normal.

'Oh, Colin, you shouldn't have. I'm coming out today.'

'I know.' He kisses her on the cheek. 'But I couldn't come here without flowers, now, could I?'

'Do you want me to put them in water for you? I'll see if I can find a vase.' The nurse takes the four bunches in her arms. 'Mrs Bliss won't be able to leave until the doctor's seen her and she's running a little late I'm afraid, but you can wait, obviously. I'll just get these sorted for you.' And she's off to fetch a vase.

'Was everything all right at home last night?' Mum's voice sounds flat.

'We're not here to talk about home, Mimi. What about you?' Colin perches on the edge of her bed. 'How are you feeling? You've given us all a terrible fright, you know.'

'I'm fine, really.' Mum doesn't look at him when she speaks but her eyes dart around the room, catching mine. 'Your brother came home last night, I trust?'

I nod. 'About tennish. He was going to come this morning but he never actually made it out of his bed.'

'You know The Boy David,' my stepfather laughs, uneasily.

'I worry about him,' sighs Mum. 'He drinks too much.'

'The only person you need to worry about right now is yourself, Miriam. I hate seeing you in here. Just promise me you're going to get better and we can put all of this behind us. Let me make it up to you, Mimi. Promise me. I know I owe you big time.'

Mum is silent as the nurse comes back with the flowers crammed into an ugly, glass vase.

'I've never been a fan of hospitals,' Mum says distantly. 'It's so difficult to sleep with all these sick people around you.'

'That's my girl.' Colin pats her hand. 'You'll be all right once we get you back into your own home. Jesus, how long do you have to wait to see a bloody doctor around here?' He gets to his feet and paces around. 'I expect you have to be on your last legs before one of them gets off their fat consultant arses.'

'I should think I'll be seeing the junior doctor,' Mum sighs.

Colin looks at her. He doesn't like to be corrected but he bites his tongue. Mum looks away.

'They're rushed off their feet and I don't suppose I'm exactly a priority case.'

'Don't make excuses for them, Miriam,' Colin snaps, then catches himself. 'You're too soft for your own good sometimes. People'll walk all over you if you give them half a chance.'

Which I guess would be funny if it weren't so damn sad.

Twenty-seven

Subject: Re. Secrets
From: Angel
Your message saddened me because, as a mother with a young son myself, I believe that too often we don't think about the effects our mistakes have on our children. You have a right to live your own life without feeling guilty. Tell your mother how you feel. Your words may be the trigger she needs to make the change. I will pray for you.

Subject: Re. Secrets
From: Lady-in-red
You poor baby. I'll bet you are tearing yourself up with feelings of guilt and anger and fear but none of this is your fault, and no: you are not a bad person. You have your own life to lead too. It's hard to see things properly when you are in the middle of them, but perhaps you could talk to someone else, face-to-face — a teacher, or a friend.

> This is not your secret. Keeping quiet
> only gives the abuser the power he
> needs to continue. Your mother will
> hopefully come to realise this in her
> own time. You must stay strong if you
> are to help her, so look after yourself
> first, learn to love yourself and then
> when your mother gets to the point
> where she realises what she must do,
> you will be strong enough to support
> her. Best wishes.

It's late in the afternoon and the warmth has already disappeared from the air. I leave the park and run along North Bridge Road, heading towards Lisa's. I can feel my pace slowing the nearer I get, but I know this is something I need to do. In four days it'll be the start of a new year. New beginnings. It's time for things to change.

'Hello, stranger!' Her mother holds the door open for me. 'You look like you could do with a drink of water.' She goes into the kitchen and fetches me a glass.

'Is Lisa around?' I can feel my face burning from the run.

As if on cue, music starts thumping through the ceiling and her mother rolls her eyes, the same way Lisa always does.

'Just follow the noise,' she sighs. 'And tell her to turn that racket down!'

I go upstairs, knock several times on the door but doubt very much that she can even hear me. Eventually I am forced to open the door myself. Lisa jumps when she sees me.

'I did knock,' I yell as she lunges for the CD player and turns it down a couple of hundred decibels.

'Jesus, this is a surprise. I was thinking of calling you anyway. What are you doing tomorrow night?'

'Tomorrow? Oh, I don't know, really. Things are kind of up in the air at the moment.'

'What, with Ian?'

Ian. I haven't even thought about him in days. I suddenly feel guilty – he probably deserves better from a girlfriend.

'Hey, I've got a phone now,' I tell her, changing the subject. 'I brought my number over for you.' I pull out one of the free sticky labels that came with it.

'Oh, excellent, Bri. Now we can call each other whenever we want. Give us a look.'

But I haven't brought it with me. Lisa looks at me as if I'm stupid. 'Well, what good is a mobile phone if you don't carry it with you?'

I shrug, reluctant to explain that I want to keep it for real emergencies.

'So did you have a good Christmas? Get anything decent?'

I shrug again. Christmas seems like a lifetime ago. Lisa shows me a couple of the things she picked up over the holidays and I pace nervously around her room. Finally, I sink down onto the bed, one of her new sweaters in my hands.

'Actually, now that you ask, Christmas was pretty shit really. I...' I very nearly back out. 'That's kind of why I came over. I... I want to talk to you, Lise.'

'I'm all ears,' she quips. 'That's why I wear my hair like this.'

'This is serious. I need to tell you something serious.'

Her face changes slightly, dark eyes searching mine. I take a deep breath in, but somehow the words won't come.

'Is it about Ian?' she prompts.

I shake my head and take another long breath. I'm actually starting to tremble. 'It's about my mum.'

Lisa nods gently. 'Still having problems, huh?'

'Yeah, but it's more than that. It's about me too, about everything in fact, about how you keep saying I've changed, everything.' I stop. 'And I need you to promise me that you won't tell anyone, not even Francine and Aysha.'

Lisa's face is grave. She nods. My hands are warm and clammy.

'Colin, my stepfather,' I begin. Lisa's eyes are getting wider. I can sense her sudden fear and wonder what she expects me to say. 'He, well, I told you that he and my mum are having problems, but, you know, it's way more than that.' I pause, twisting my hands round and round the jumper, tying it in knots. 'About two years ago he started to get violent, usually with Mum, once or twice with me. He bashes her. She ended up in hospital on Boxing Day. I'm scared that one day he's going to kill her. I want her to leave him but I don't think she will.' The words are coming thick and fast now. 'She's scared of him. We all are, because we never know how he's going to be from one day to the next. The reason our phone doesn't work any more is because he smashed it over Mum's head. That's why I don't come out any more, Lise. That's why I don't invite you over. That's why. And now you know.'

I glance up at her. Her face is white. I take a long steadying breath and try and slow down the thumping in my chest.

'You said he was *strict*, Bri. I didn't think – '

'I was too scared to say anything before. I thought it might make things worse, or you might think I was making things up or something. I don't know. After a while you just get used to keeping your mouth shut.'

Lisa swallows hard. 'I don't know what to say, Bri.'

'You don't have to say anything. I just wanted to tell you, to explain.'

'But, Bri, I don't know if, I mean, this is a lot bigger than, say, you and Ian getting it on or something... I mean this is *big*. I don't think I can keep this to myself.'

I stiffen, suddenly frightened that I've set something in motion that I won't be able to stop. Lisa sees the panic in my face.

'Maybe I can tell my mum. I just don't know if I can keep all of this inside me. My mum's not one for blabbing and she doesn't really know your mother, does she? It's not like she'll say anything.'

It seems mad to me. I've kept this secret for the last two years and now Lisa wants to tell the whole world within five minutes. She seems to read my mind.

'My mum won't breathe a word to anyone, Bri, I promise.'

'Yeah, but she'll look at me differently.' I mumble. 'It won't feel the same.'

But then again, that's why I've told Lisa, isn't it? So that things aren't going to be the same. So that I'm not buying into the same secrets and lies as my mother.

I sigh, feel the fight draining out of me. It's like undoing a pair of jeans that are way too tight – you can feel your insides relaxing, slowly spreading out into their natural shape again. I'd forgotten how tightly I hold myself in. Lisa smiles at me then gives me a hug. And, in a small way, everything *is* different, for the first time in ages.

Twenty-eight

Come Monday, Colin is reluctant to leave Mum alone but she insists she will be fine, that he can't be with her 24-7 and he begrudgingly allows himself to be talked into going back to work.

'I might come home at lunch-time.' He kisses her. 'Just to check on you.'

She turns her face. 'There's no need.'

'You know I worry about you, I can't help myself. And I don't suppose there'll be much to do in the office, this is always a dead time of year.'

'Go!' she sighs. 'I'll be fine, I promise.'

When his car has reversed out of the drive and we hear the engine dying away down Lavender Avenue she gets up from the table and starts clearing away the breakfast dishes. I take them from her.

'I can do this. You sit back down.'

'Bri, I'm not an invalid, as I keep telling everyone.'

'You've been in hospital!'

'I know that. And I'm out now. Why don't you go out and see your boyfriend? Do something fun for a change.'

'I've got homework to do,' I lie.

'I don't want you staying in on my account,' Mum

tells me. 'I'm going to be fine. I just need a bit of time to myself right now.'

I look at her and can feel tears gathering at the back of my throat. I want to hug her but know that it will only hurt her.

I go for a run instead but my energy levels are way down and my legs start to shake before I've even completed a full lap of the park. I slow to a walk, looking at the rushing river beside me, still swollen with rainwater. That night when Ian and I pulled Amy out of there seems like an eternity ago. I take my mobile phone out of my pocket and begin a message.

```
Sorry nt bn around more. Thngs
complicated at home. Don't try n call.
Whn I come back 2 school promise 2
tell U evrythg. Happy New Year.
Briony.
```

It takes me as long to work out what is acceptable shorthand for texting as it would to punch in the full words but I want to get it right. Then I switch off my phone in case he calls me back. I feel like a sorry excuse for a girlfriend but I just can't deal with everything at the moment. First, I've got to spend a bit more time on myself.

When I get back home, Mum is where I left her, sitting at the kitchen table, staring quietly into space.

'Mum? What's going on?'

'I'm thinking.'

A shiver runs over my skin as I register the bottle of pills in her hand. 'What about?'

She doesn't answer me.

'Mum? You're not thinking about... well, doing

anything stupid?' It hurts me to say the words but she's scaring me, just sitting there, like a zombie.

'You mean more stupid than I have already?' she asks without moving her head.

'Mum, you're frightening me.'

'Life *is* frightening, Briony.'

She turns her head to look at me. Her face looks different somehow and it has nothing to do with the yellowing bruises, which mark her like tattoos.

'I guess it's time I took a good hard look at my life, isn't it?'

I shrug. 'Maybe, I suppose. I don't know.'

'Bri, can I ask you something?' she whispers. 'If I left, would you come with me?'

I have to hold the chair to stop me from falling on my face. The floor spins wildly under my feet. 'Leave? You mean leave Colin? Leave here?'

She nods, just once, then falls silent.

'Like a shot, Mum, of course I would. What about David?'

'What about him? He's all grown up, he can look after himself. He told me as much yesterday.' Mum turns back to the table and her eyes are full of hurt. I silently curse him. 'What about school?'

'I don't know. How far are you planning to move?'

'I don't know. That's just it, there are so many things I don't know.' She turns back to me. 'Don't go making any rash plans, Briony. It was just a thought. I've got a lot of things on my mind right now. I just wondered how you felt about it, that's all.'

'But you know how I feel, Mum,' I say urgently. 'I've told you time and time again. I hate what Colin does to you. I hate him and I hate this house.'

I draw a deep breath but instantly I can see that I've gone too far. She sighs and turns away. I stare down at my trainers, wishing that I'd just kept my big mouth shut. Probably I'm not the only one who feels like they're being ripped down the middle.

Twenty-nine

'Briony.' Colin catches me on the stairs coming back from a late-night run.

I tense, wondering what I've done wrong this time. He coughs to clear his throat, speaks in a low voice, won't look me in the eye.

'I think I owe you an apology,' he starts, 'for what happened, last week.'

I stare at him. He coughs again, glances around awkwardly as if he is scared of being overheard.

'Anyway, I was hoping we could put it behind us, you know, new year, new start for all of us? I probably don't deserve to ask, but I'm going to make it up to your mum and I'll make it up to you, too. What do you say?'

Words stick in my throat. Don't you dare make it up to her. Don't you dare fob her off with more of your lies. You have no right to ask anything of us.

'Briony?' he prompts.

My stomach wretches. 'Sorry. I don't feel so good.' I mutter and hurl myself upstairs towards the toilet.

They're making plans for tomorrow, New Year's Eve. Mum's only been out of hospital for four days and already it's like nothing's happened. I keep thinking it's my fault, for pushing her too hard. Maybe I've scared her off.

Mum's face is strained into a tight smile as she listens to Colin's plans. He wants to take her somewhere posh for a meal.

'It's a new start for us, Mimi,' he tells her. 'I want to show you that I'm serious about making things right for you again.'

'I know.' She nods.

He pulls a cell phone out of his briefcase and keys in his PIN number. I had no idea he had a mobile.

For the next ten minutes he sits in his armchair with the local paper spread over his knees, phoning round restaurants, but, of course, most of them have been booked up for weeks already. Eventually he slings the phone down, crumples up the paper and chucks it on the floor.

'It doesn't matter, Col. We can stay in. I haven't anything to wear anyway.' Mum says.

Colin has a sour look on his face. 'Whole bloody world is against me, that's what. I try to make things better but nobody wants me to succeed, do they? Not really. They all want to see me fall on my face.'

'I'm just as happy staying in,' Mum's voice quivers. She glances up at Colin as he storms out of his chair and goes to put the kettle on.

An uneasy calm descends over the living room in his absence. The knot is back under my ribs. Mum sighs and reaches for the TV guide. She looks sad.

'I'll do some washing later,' she tells me without looking up. 'Put out anything you might want.'

And though she doesn't say anything else, I kind of know what she means.

Thirty

Go to work. Go to work you miserable sod. Get off your bastard arse and just go to work. I hold my head in my hands to concentrate the thoughts more, sending them across the breakfast table to Colin as he mulls over the day's news in his morning paper. David has already gone to work, to fit tyres. Then he'll probably end up down the pub, just as he did last year, and the year before that. Nothing changes unless you *make* it change. This morning Mum gave him an extra sandwich and a vanilla and cherry slice, but he never even noticed.

Colin turns the news pages lazily, takes another sip of his coffee, scanning the columns for things that interest him.

'What are you up to today?' he asks me suddenly.

I jump. I had been so busy concentrating on his departure that I had forgotten to act the way I normally do.

'Oh, the usual. Just a bit of homework and maybe a run in the park.' I dump my plate in the sink and shoot Mum a quick look.

'Shouldn't you be going to work, love?' She wipes the table in front of him.

He glances up. Does he look suspicious or am I just getting paranoid? 'You sound like you want to get rid of me, Miriam.'

Mum laughs stiffly. 'I just want to get started on the cleaning, fresh start for a new year and all that.'

I hold my breath, waiting to see how he reacts. Mum turns to me. 'Briony, go and brush your teeth. I don't want you lazing around the house all day.' Her voice sounds strange to my ears. She turns back to Colin. 'And that goes for you too!'

Colin closes his paper and gets to his feet, puts his coffee cup in the sink, and kisses my mother on the head.

'Bossy women, eh? What's the world coming to? Okay, Miriam, you win.' He kisses her again. 'I'll get some wine for tonight on the way home. Don't do anything I wouldn't while I'm gone.'

His words send a shiver down my back.

I follow him upstairs, take longer than usual in the bathroom, wait until I hear the front door slam and the car rev out of the drive before I sprint out of there and tear into my bedroom. I see Mum dart past the open door. She still holds her side when she moves too fast, momentarily forgetting about the broken ribs Colin's left her with.

I shove my school kit into a bag, zip up the lumpy holdall I filled last night, and then sit on the edge of the bed and look around me. There is nothing here I will be sad to leave behind. Mum appears moments later with two small suitcases.

'That was quick.'

She pushes a cab firm's card towards me. 'Call them, will you?' She looks around the room.

'Where do I say we're going?'

'The station. We're going to Cath's.' She glances back at me. 'And make it quick, before I change my mind.'

I leap off the bed, limbs trembling.

The taxi will be ten minutes. I wonder if ten minutes is long enough to change your entire life. We go downstairs, sit in the front room, peep through the nets, waiting for our cab to arrive.

'It feels weird,' I say, trying to blot out the relentless ticking of the clock on the wall.

'I guess I'm not being fair on you, am I, Bri? This is your GCSE year as well.' Mum's voice is pained.

Panic starts to rise within me. 'It's not a problem, Mum. Honestly.'

'We'll sort it out, won't we, Bri?' She wants me to tell her she's doing the right thing so I nod, tell her yes, tell her anything she needs to hear, anything to get her away from this place.

It must have been ten minutes by now. Where's the taxi got to? The hands on the clock have barely inched round six minutes.

'I feel bad about leaving David like this,' Mum sighs, watching a car that isn't a cab go past the window. 'I know he's going to stay with friends but it's not the same...'

'He's a big boy now. He can look after himself,' I say. 'Anyway, once we're settled he can come and stay with us if he wants. You know David though...' And I leave it at that because it suddenly occurs to me that none of us really know David any more. But then I also think, he was the first one to leave. Sometimes you don't have to physically change place to leave your home behind.

I daren't even ask her what plans she's made. When we get settled. Where? Cath's will be fine for a week or so but what next? I don't want to ask in case the details frighten her back into her shell. I don't want to push her too hard, but now I'm starting to panic. Maybe she hasn't got *anything* planned at all. I see us both sitting at Cath's all day until she finally cracks and rings Colin to take us home again. I sneak a look at her. She is staring determinedly out of the window.

'Of course, I'm still going to have to face him sooner or later,' she says into the nets.

'Who? Colin?'

She nods. 'He won't like it. I could be making things a lot worse, you know.' She looks at me and the silence hangs between us. She's right. It won't end here.

Another car cruises past but doesn't stop.

'Let's hope Col hasn't forgotten anything today...' Mum lets slip a nervous laugh.

I turn desperately back to the clock. Nine minutes. Ten minutes. Eleven minutes. Twelve. Mum flinches at the window. A car honks its horn.

'It's here!' she gasps.

I leap to my feet so quickly that it makes me dizzy but I stumble out to the hallway with my luggage, not about to let on to Mum.

'Got everything?'

We are both standing at the front door. The sun is streaming through the stained glass panels at the top throwing shapes over the walls. I nod. Mum picks up her cases, a slight pain from her side catching her as she does so.

I turn the catch on the door and the cold, crisp air pushes up against us. At the bottom of the path the cabbie is getting out of his taxi, looking at us with our bags and cases.

'Here, I'll give you a hand,' he calls, heading up to join us as we step gingerly through into the sunlight. 'Nice day for it.'

He takes Mum's cases from her. She teeters slightly without their weight to balance her and puts her hand on my shoulder.

'We'll be okay, Bri,' she whispers.
We head towards the waiting taxi.
'Yeah, I know we will.'
We'll be okay. We have to be.